MW00478336

TRANSSEXUAL APOSTATE

TRANSSEXUAL APOSTATE

My Journey Back to Reality

DEBBIE HAYTON

FORUM

FORUM

First published in Great Britain by Forum, an imprint of Swift Press 2024

1 3 5 7 9 8 6 4 2

Printed and bound in Great Britain by CPI Group (UK) Ltd,
Croydon, CRO 4YY
A CIP catalogue record for this book is available from the British Library

ISBN: 9781800753099
eISBN: 9781800753105

MIX
Paper | Supporting
responsible forestry
FSC
www.fsc.org   FSC® C171272

CONTENTS

Prologue: Gender Reassignment   1

1 Growing Up   11

2 Trans Orthodoxy   29

3 Awakening   49

4 Autogynephilia   71

5 Perception and Reality   93

6 Gender Identity to Gender Apostasy   117

7 Apostasy and Exclusion   139

8 TERF Island: Britain against the World   161

9 Children and Technology   181

10 The Transsexual Future   203

Epilogue: Another Perspective, by Stephanie Hayton   215

ACKNOWLEDGEMENTS   225

NOTES   227

To my family

PROLOGUE

GENDER REASSIGNMENT

After a flurry of activity there was a pause and a question. 'Are you sure you want to do this?' I was already hooked up, and I was about to be plumbed in. White cables connected the sticky dots on my chest to the stack of electronics, while a cannula in the back of my left hand awaited the piping that dangled from a drip. The consent forms had already been signed but the anaesthetist gave me one final chance to get up and walk out of the room, fit and seemingly healthy.

Gender reassignment surgery (GRS) is a major procedure. The genitals are sliced open and repurposed. Skin from the scrotum becomes the labia, while a neoclitoris is constructed from part of the glans. The newly constructed cavity that will become the neovagina is then lined with skin from the penis. The urethra is shortened and repositioned. Finally, the new cavity is packed with cotton wool and everything is then stitched up before a compression dressing is fitted to hold it all together for the next five days.

If everything goes to plan, the surgeon can create an aesthetic and functional facsimile of female genitalia. But much can go wrong. I had been warned about failures in the carpentry, the plumbing and the electrics. Most seriously, that new cavity can lead to a recto-neovaginal fistula that I was told would be 'difficult to treat'. Complications in the waterworks include renal and urinary infections, while swellings can lead to blockages. Some problems clear up with antibiotics and the passage of time, but incontinence can be permanent. Finally, sexual function relies on nerves reconnecting, something I was told fails in maybe 20 per cent of cases.

The anaesthetist's question was pertinent, but my mind was made up: 'Yes, go for it!' He reassured me that I should not feel any pain afterwards but the compression dressing might be uncomfortable. Trussed up like a chicken, he said. Immobility was likely to be a bigger issue. Four days of enforced bed rest can lead to back pain. Immediately after surgery I would have a morphine line that I could click on demand. He encouraged me to use it.

It was three minutes past three in the afternoon. A syringe of colourless liquid appeared – a 'strong painkiller', I was told. In a flash, the contents disappeared into the cannula. Two seconds later peace and calm filled my brain, while a mask appeared in front of my face. Fresh air, they said. I didn't believe that for a moment, but I was already too far gone to argue. I breathed deeply and left them to it.

Twenty-four hours earlier I was sitting in a coffee shop in west London pondering the future. Sunday afternoon,

14 February 2016. Check-in time at Charing Cross Hospital was four o'clock, so I had time to reflect. I had been thinking about this operation for a long time: 101 weeks had elapsed since my referral for surgery. The delay was frustrating but, as an NHS patient, I took my place in line. Demand had been increasing and the hospital had limited resources.

However, with just one day to go, I struggled to articulate to myself why I needed to go through with the procedure. I was still convinced that I was some kind of woman, and I needed the operation in order to live authentically as a woman – whatever that might mean. But it didn't make rational sense, it felt more like a matter of faith.

I finished my coffee and walked down the Fulham Palace Road to the hospital. After being buzzed through two locked doors, I was asked to take a seat. Something I still took for granted. I had been warned by those who had gone before that it would be some weeks before I could sit comfortably again.

Check-in was followed by dinner, and outside the sky went dark. There was more time to think. My family was scattered: Stephanie – my wife – was at home in Birmingham, while our daughter was a student in Leeds. Meanwhile, our two sons were on their way to spend the half-term week with my mother-in-law in Middlesbrough. I was not expecting any family visitors in London.

It was a long evening and a longer morning. I was nil-by-mouth from 6 a.m. As the day wore on, I learned that the surgeon was running late and I just had to wait. There were messages from home. Stephanie was brief: 'Presume you'll be going down soon. Hope all goes ok. Thanks for phoning earlier. Speak to you later.' My summons finally came at quarter to three. I was dispatched from the ward on foot, accompanied by a nurse. We go into this surgery fit and healthy, and certainly capable of getting there under our own steam.

I walked in but I was wheeled out. Consciousness returned gradually in recovery. The anaesthetist was right: there was a second cannula in my hand. A saline drip in one and the promised morphine line in the other. I asked the time – it was just after 7 p.m. The surgery had taken four hours. I had been expecting two to three. What did that mean? But I was too tired to worry about it. There was indeed no pain and I drifted in and out of sleep as my bed was pushed through the hospital.

After thirteen long hours I ordered tea with extra sugar. I messaged Stephanie as I sipped my tea: 'Hiya. I love you.' As Stephanie relayed the news to the children, I asked for some food. The drip was devoid of calories and I was hungry. I tried the morphine clicker but it was my stomach that demanded attention.

I did not move from that bed for four days. Food came morning, noon and night, while a catheter dealt with the outflow. The liquid part, that was. The other function was a bigger concern for me – I was patched up and stitched together – but the nurse shrugged: 'You've had enough morphine to keep that quiet for a few days.' I gave it another click for good measure. Remarkably, I could still feel my old anatomy. During GRS, body parts are harvested and replanted elsewhere. My brain had not yet registered that familiar signals were now coming from new locations.

My biggest problem was boredom, but across the ward there were troubles of a different kind. Another GRS patient was bleeding, and the flimsy curtains offered little privacy. I could hear everything. For half an hour, two nurses failed to stem the flow. The surgeon was called urgently; she applied a cement and the bleeding stopped. The patient asked what they would have done if the cement had not worked. The surgeon was brief: 'The cement will work.' If there had been a plan B, the surgeon did not share it with her patient. Two days earlier we had both walked in here; we now lay helpless. I checked my own dressing; it was dry.

The following day, the specialist nurse delivered two vaginal dilators. For the time being I was packed up and sealed – quite literally – but on Saturday, five days after surgery, the cotton wool would be removed from the neovagina and dilation would have to begin. A lining of penile skin keeps the open wound from healing, but the cavity needs to be dilated regularly, three times per day in the days and weeks after surgery. Eight years on, that has become a weekly activity. Perhaps as well since a dilation routine takes half an hour at least.

There were two dilators, both about 20 cm long and made from hard transparent plastic. The thinner one – 25 mm in diameter – would go in first. For about five minutes, I was told. The fatter one – 30 mm across – then needed a quarter of an hour. The extra 5 mm didn't sound much, but the cross-sectional area was half as much again. But that maths lesson was for another day.

By the time Saturday morning came, I was already mobile. A leg bag had been fitted to the catheter on the Friday, and I could empty it myself and measure the contents in the jug provided. But causing me much greater concern were my bowels – they had not been emptied for four days. Laxatives were added to my medication sheet on Friday morning. There was a backlog to clear, and I worried about what was stitched up under the dressing. If the sutures gave way, the neovagina might prolapse and probably be wrecked in the process.

Richter 10 came and went, and my body survived the experience. But I made a mess of the catheter line and sterile dressings. Help came. A week earlier I had been busy at work; now I was lying on my back being cleaned up by nursing staff. That was Friday afternoon. The unpacking was scheduled for the next morning when there would be only one specialist ward nurse on duty. She told me to be ready at 9 a.m.

It tickled – as I had been warned – but it was tickling like nothing I have ever felt before, and coming from a location my brain could not place. The first dilator went in. Five inches, the specialist nurse said, and it took a good five minutes to get it there despite the lashings of lubricant. The second dilator was harder. Ten minutes to insert, but as soon as it was in place, the nurse was called away. Just hold it there, I was told.

But I was not ready for the pain that built up when that 30-mm dilator was inserted into an open wound 5 inches deep. After eighteen minutes I could take no more and pulled it out. There was blood, goo and a piece of hard plastic. I buzzed for help. An agency nurse took one look and backed away. I felt very alone. The specialist nurse returned thirty-five minutes after she had left. She apologised for leaving me but she explained that since it was a Saturday, she was the only regular nurse on the ward. For the staff, this was routine.

The cannulas also came out on the Saturday, and the catheter in the middle of Sunday night. Freed from my external plumbing, I was then ready to be discharged on Monday, eight days after I had walked in. But first I needed to work out how to urinate again. It was not straightforward. My groin was swollen and the muscles seemed to work differently. I was sent into the bathroom with a jug, and I returned triumphant with 275 ml of clear yellow liquid.

The surgeon popped in to 'check the wound'. He seemed happy enough with it. The specialist nurse checked my dilation technique and told me that I was ready to be discharged. The carpentry was fine; the electrics I knew I needed to wait for. My concern was the plumbing. The call of nature was getting harder to answer. But I was keen to get home and reassured myself that as long as I could get a few drops out, there was probably nothing more to come. That was a big mistake.

Eight days earlier I navigated the Underground, striding through the tunnels to make the connection at Green Park station. The return journey to Euston and my home in Birmingham was far more sedate. I shuffled to the taxi and sat gingerly on a foam cushion. My pelvic floor was in tatters and I felt every bump. On the train, I failed to pass any water. It was warm, though. Maybe I was dehydrated?

It was good to be home. I was pleased to see Stephanie and the boys. Home cooking beat the offerings from the hospital trolley, and, following medical advice, it was washed down with 'plenty of fluids'. Then it was time for the next dilation routine. For the first time there was no button to summon a nurse, but I had already become adept in the administration of plastic rods. But a rather more basic function eluded me. Despite drinking water by the pint glass, the outflow had fallen to zero.

As discomfort morphed into agony, I feared that my bladder might rupture. With no call button to press, Stephanie drove me to A & E in Birmingham. Traffic was light and we were there in ten minutes. After eight days in one hospital, I was standing in the triage line in another. This place was heaving. After ten minutes I was deemed to be non-urgent and told to wait. The hard chairs were not an option so I stood. After what felt like hours, but was actually thirty minutes, a nurse took a look.

'Please can you put a catheter in? I'm bursting.' She said no. I suggested I might call an ambulance: 'The paramedics will catheterise me if you won't.'

'Not a week after GRS they wouldn't,' she retorted. 'You will just need to wait.' It was well past midnight when I was taken to a treatment cubicle. Stephanie went home to the boys while a nurse set up an ultrasound machine. 'If there's more than 150 ml in there, they will probably put a catheter in,' he advised. From what I could see, the reading was 999+. I enquired what that meant. He grimaced. 'Over a litre! No wonder you're suffering.'

Pain relief was increased from paracetamol to gas and air, Entonox – the stuff Stephanie was given in childbirth. That at least took my mind off things. But I was summoned back to reality by a new voice. 'Hello, I'm the all-night plumber, I hear you have a blockage.' He was the on-call urologist. He took the gas away – 'You are going to make yourself sick' – and swiftly inserted a catheter.

There was brief comedy in the cubicle when they could not find a bag for the other end. But within seconds, a large one was found. Ten minutes later, it contained 1,300 ml. 'Seriously impressive', according to the nurse. Less than twenty-four hours after being discharged from one hospital, I was admitted to another. Bloods were taken – to see if the blockage had backed up into my kidneys and damaged them – and a bed was found. It was three in the morning, but the next dilation was due. I went to sleep at four.

There was no lie-in. My bloods were fine, and the hospital needed the bed. After speaking with the specialist nurse at Charing Cross, they told me that blockages were not uncommon and to give it more time with the catheter. But I should watch for infections: 'It was a bit of a mess down there.' So after one more dilation routine, I was fitted with another leg bag and discharged into the care of my GP. Stephanie drove me home.

I saw my surgeon one final time, two months after surgery. He was happy with his work, and dismissive of my problems: 'These things happen,' he said. Gender reassignment surgery is a major procedure, and positive outcomes rely at least in part on patients being fit and healthy when they walk into the anaesthetic room. But the results are not always as hoped. Cobbling something together from spare parts can never replicate the genuine article.

Even so, patients queue up for it and the National Health Service pays for it. Received wisdom is that it is a necessary treatment for gender dysphoria, but what is gender dysphoria? Eight years on from that surgery, I now wonder. In 2016, I was convinced I had to put myself through life-changing treatment to restore my mental health. Why? Previous generations seemed to manage without it. But to answer that question we need to start at the very beginning, for me at least: April 1968.

I

GROWING UP

M y childhood was unremarkable. But since it's the only childhood I can remember, it's hard to judge. I was introverted – I was quite happy with my own company – but I would hardly have been described as asocial. I grew up in a loving family – with two younger brothers – and I had all the friends I needed. My interest in science blossomed early and, while my parents might not have expected me to join the teaching profession, they would not have been surprised that my speciality was physics. By the age of seven, my shelves were filling up with books about astronomy and space exploration. Perhaps I was a bit odd, but, to the outside world at least, my interests were stereotypically male. I played with construction kits; I even had a set of trucks.

Internally, I struggled. But doesn't everyone? Life is a new experience for every young child, and the novelty is not limited to the external world. In some ways coping with external matters is easy: they go away when we close our eyes and stick our fingers in our ears. But the internal world is always there. Our brains are the result of a billion years of evolution, and instinct is pre-installed within them. Nobody teaches us to breathe, or feel hungry, for example, and by the age of three I knew all about guilt, shame and fear.

I don't think that three-year-old boy, sitting on the floor in his front room, would have been able to articulate the meaning of those words, but he knew how to feel the emotions they described. I was learning to count beyond twenty. My earliest memories date from the previous year, and those snippets were also seasoned with very strong emotions: guilt when I broke my grandmother's clock; fear when my parents encouraged me to make friends with a boy I did not know; and a sense of loss when we moved house. But on that day in 1971 I was overwhelmed with a feeling that I have since labelled as shame.

Over fifty years later I cannot only picture the scene – I can still feel it. A family friend introduced me to new and bigger numbers. The pattern was immediately obvious to me – thirty, forty, fifty – the mere repetition made it easy. But when we got to sixty, a chill ran down my spine. Before it happened, I knew that we would soon get to eighty – a word that sounded similar to 'tights', clothing that I knew was only for girls. Where this taboo came from, I do not know, but it had already taken up residence in my head. Clearly, I already knew the difference between boys and girls, and the clothes we wore. But – significantly – I knew that girls' clothes were forbidden to me. Instinct? It was certainly nothing I had been taught.

Clothes were an ongoing issue for me throughout child-hood. I wanted to wear girls' clothes but, at the same time, I was terrified that someone would read my thoughts. But without any sisters – or female friends, for that matter – my opportunities were limited. It was rubbish, sometimes literally. My mother would discard laddered tights, throwing them in the bin, and probably think nothing more about them. But for me they were oases in the desert. If circumstances were right, I could retrieve them before they were covered by potato peelings, soggy tea bags, or worse. But I also needed privacy to try them on, before replacing them exactly as I found them. I became obsessive about that. This was something that nobody else must ever know, including anyone else with a meticulous knowledge of the arrangement of discarded trash.

From the age of five this cycle would repeat, whether I wanted it to or not. First there was anticipation, then excitement. My heartbeat rose, and my body would become aroused. I was euphoric, though the exhilaration I felt was always tempered by the ever-present fear of discovery. Emotionally I was on a trip but, while my brain always craved for more, I had no idea how to respond to my feelings. The spell was almost always broken by worries about being discovered. As I came down from my high, I would replace everything as I found it. I was scrupulous about that. If I was ever dysphoric, it was the grief at the loss of the high.

Only once was I ever caught. Inexplicably, I had failed to lock the bathroom door. I was usually so careful about that, and my grandmother stumbled in on me. I was mortified.

She called for my parents: 'Come and look at this!' Suddenly there were three faces looking at me. Nothing more was said. What – indeed – could be said? Then the adults went away, leaving me to myself. For what felt like a long time, I sat there in shock. Without knowing what else I could do, I reverted to my usual routine and put everything back as I found it. Then I had to face what I imagined would be an inquisition in the living room. I went in with my head down, looking at the floor. I grabbed a book and engrossed myself in it. As the minutes passed, nothing was said. Had I imagined it all? I remember weighing up that possibility. But it had definitely happened, and nobody said a thing. Not then, not ever. But – like the earlier counting incident – it was seared into my memory. I was eight years old.

If my bedtime wishes had ever been granted I would have been magically turned into a girl when I woke the next morning. For a while, I prayed that when I woke, I would always have been a girl. When that hope was finally extinguished, I pitched for second best – that the magical transformation would be news, and probably a shock, to everyone. I was certainly persistent, but fantasy was not reality. That was clear to me long before puberty. I knew that my dreams were futile and, beyond my anguished musings, there was a bigger world to explore.

Had I been growing up today, I would have certainly come across the concept of 'transgender children'. Whether that knowledge would have precipitated a disclosure to my parents, I do not know. Back in the 1970s, I had a problem that I never understood. Shame gripped me tightly, and I knew that my inexplicable desire to be the other sex must be kept firmly under wraps. In many ways it was miserable but, at the same time, I was free to grow to adulthood without being socially transitioned. If that had happened, I would have been faced with the possibility of puberty blockers and then cross-sex hormones. I'm glad I was never put in that position. I was a bright boy, but I was never competent to consent to such profound treatments. Or able to face the sense of loss if the possibility passed me by.

To understand what it meant to be an adult, I had to become one. As I grew, I yearned for children of my own. There was only one way that was going to happen: nature needed to take its course. Looking back, I'm pleased it did.

Primary school offered just two opportunities for public cross-dressing. I remember them vividly. First, the village fete. I was to be a ladybird. The red papier-mâché shell that my mother spent so long making was incidental: my mind focused on the tight black jumper and the black tights. The adrenaline that ran through my body was palpable, but I was too ashamed to say anything. Also palpable was the subsequent sense of loss when my own fears stopped me from asking to keep the tights, perhaps to wear when it was cold? I was six years old.

By the time I was nine, repression gripped me even more tightly. This second opportunity was the school Christmas play: my teacher had cast me as a carol singer. For some long-forgotten reason, the boys and girls were to be dressed the same – tunics and thick tights. I could not even take that request home without deliberately garbling the message.

Alone in that group, I wore my school trousers. There was shame in being different – the odd one out – but it was preferable to the shame of articulating the thoughts that rattled incessantly inside my head.

Externally, my life was unremarkable. Despite my fears that I might sprout a thought bubble, nobody ever read my mind and I grew up without being discovered. Primary school was left behind and I navigated my way through a much larger secondary school. Science and maths came easily to me, and I was a high achiever in class. Still reserved – some aspects of our character are lifelong – I made new friends where necessary and I focused on my studies.

My internal struggles might have been sexual – they clearly related to my sex – but they were not erotic. I wasn't acting like some miniature adult: I was playing like a child. Never was my focus a relationship with a girl; instead, I wanted to *be* a girl. Certainly, until I stumbled into puberty, the hormone that drove me was not testosterone, but adrenaline. The mere thought of being a girl gave me the rush; writing it down in a diary focused it. Coupled with the fear of my words being discovered, I rode an emotional rollercoaster alone inside my head.

Puberty brings changes in everyone. Physically, my response to testosterone was textbook. I grew rapidly, sprouted hair and developed spots, and my voice broke. All rather normal and reassuring, starting bang on time around age thirteen. I had mixed feelings about puberty, but relief featured strongly. I had harboured genuine worries that I was so strange, puberty would not happen to me. Perhaps

I was totally unique in my cross-sex identification, and if that were true then what else was different about me? The alternative – or so it seemed to me at the time – was that every boy felt as I did, but nobody talked about it, and I could never ask. But, looking back, I think both ideas were wrong. I now believe that I was developing a psychological condition called autogynephilia, which affects maybe 1 to 3 per cent of men. We are unusual, but far from unique.

At the time, however, I was navigating the process of growing up to be a man. One thing didn't change, though: my internal experience seemed different from that of my male friends. While they began to take an interest in girls, my desire to be a girl intensified from a want to a need and ultimately an insatiable compulsion. The maelstrom of emotions inside my head had to find a focus somewhere, and it was buying clothes. If I couldn't actually be a girl – and by then I had given up wishing for magic – I could try to clothe my body to at least create an illusion.

At fourteen, I bought my first pair of tights from a newsagent on my way home from school. My cover story was well rehearsed – I was on an errand, of course – but my heart was in my mouth when I handed over my money. This was like the bathroom experiences of my primary-school days, but much more intense – it was now public and other people were involved. Not that the newsagent seemed to care. My money was just as good as anyone else's. Was the manic thumping of my heart the same as what my male friends experienced when they asked a girl out? I didn't know because I never asked.

I bought other clothes as well, though I took no more risks in local shops where I might have been recognised. I took trips to other towns but, even then, I shuddered with the fear of discovery. Secret purchases needed to be well hidden, and I became very good at that. But the adrenaline was now supplemented by testosterone, and that drove a need for sexual release. I started the first of many cycles. Ultimately each one was as futile as the one before it. Sexual release brought self-disgust, and regularly that was strong enough to lead to a purge of my secret wardrobe. Had I kept all the girls' clothes I bought, I would never have been able to find the space to hide them. I was in a mental whirlpool, and I simply had no idea how to control the powerful emotions that held me captive.

Despite my inner turmoil, I did well at school. My family were proud of me when I departed for university, and later secured a degree in Astronomy and Astrophysics. Suddenly I had the freedom of living away from home, but the inner chains never relaxed and the cycles of purging continued. What if the cleaner found my skirt? Looking back, I guess that the cleaner wouldn't have cared even if she'd realised that it was mine. The logical conclusion, of course, would have been that a girlfriend had left it in my room.

But even as an undergraduate I had no girlfriends. I didn't know how to relate to myself; pursuing interests in the other sex was beyond me. But although my immediate physical needs were satisfied with my bag of clothes – always strictly alone – human beings are social animals. We need relationships, and I was no exception. I am heterosexual – I am a male person who is sexually attracted to females – and love is far more than lust. Like other heterosexual males, evolution had put within me a need for a girlfriend to share my life with. But it would take someone very special to break me free from my inner world.

The first time I set eyes on Stephanie, I was blown away. By then I had completed my first degree, and was just about to embark on a PhD. She was starting the second year of a physics degree in the same department. She was nineteen; I was twenty-one. Love at first sight is a cliché, and in my case it was also one-sided. My initial overtures were rebuffed. She was happy to be friends but not looking for a relationship with me. And then she started going out with someone else.

Stephanie was a Christian and, since we had become friends, her friends became my friends. Before too much longer, her faith became my faith. For a time, my intellectual energies were devoted to the reconciliation of my new faith in God with my long-standing faith in science. That, however, was a mere academic exercise compared to a rather greater contradiction in my life. At first glance, at least, the Bible was clear. According to Deuteronomy 22:5: 'A woman must not wear men's clothing, nor a man wear women's clothing, for the Lord your God detests anyone who does this.'

However, it was not the Bible that kept me from coming out as a transvestite – or even a transsexual – in the early 1990s. Nor – with hindsight – was it the people around me, or society at large. The person who maintained the lock on those inner chains was me. I told nobody because I did not want to tell anybody. Cross-dressing remained a secret endeavour, and one that I tried to end with every purge. I desperately wanted it all to stop so I could be like everyone else – or, at least, like my perception of others. The possibility that other people had issues of their own passed me by.

Fifteen months after I first met Stephanie, I was convinced that I had achieved normality. We grew closer, and, in December 1990, we became an 'item' – in the language of the student world. We introduced each other to our respective families: this was a serious relationship. The internal struggle that I had battled since the age of three had waxed and waned over the years, but suddenly it was gone. I no longer wanted to be a girl – I had a girl. Stephanie was twenty and she was perfect in every way. She was not only beautiful, she was also a physicist. Life could not have been better for me. We talked about the possibility of marriage and a future together. I purged my secret bag of clothes for the last time and finally broke the cycle.

Or so I thought: the relief I enjoyed did not last. Our relationship brought remission rather than cure. Within months, the internal strife returned. But this time, I was determined to focus on Stephanie rather than myself. Something easier said than done – I have likened my desire to become the other sex to holding down a beach ball underwater. Get it in the right position and it can stay down without affecting life on the surface. But there was more to it than that: I needed to keep it hidden as well. My problem may have been mental rather than physical, but it was hard work all the same. And is it fair to keep something so profound secret from someone you are planning to marry? I thought not, so I had to say something.

Up until that time – I was twenty-three – I had told nobody. The thought of sharing something so personal and shameful filled me with terror. The fear of rejection was real, but the biggest hurdle was internal. Before I could explain my secret to others, I needed to admit it to myself, and to do that I needed to find the words to describe it.

The terminology was there: 'transsexual' and 'transvestite' were used and understood, and they were familiar to me. In the years before the internet, I had spent hours sitting alone in the city library reading about them. Perhaps other people took those books home, but I could never put them on my library card. If the computer system knew what I had been reading, then maybe human beings might know as well. My need for secrecy had been obsessive. No, it was better to stay in the library and put the books back on the shelf when nobody was looking.

I learned that transsexuals were pitied while transvestites were objects of ridicule. That was clear from TV – the television, that is – of my childhood. Comedians such as Dick Emery, Melvyn Hayes and even the Two Ronnies would cross-dress for laughs. Sometimes there were sexual overtones. At the time homosexuality was unspeakable, at least before the 9 p.m. watershed, so effeminate behaviour could be a proxy. John Inman's character in *Are You Being Served?* would joke about it: when admiring women's clothes, he would announce that he was the same size as his mother. I watched these programmes transfixed. But they were a world away from the one I lived in, and, besides, I was neither effeminate nor gay. That I was confident about: the focus of my interest was Stephanie and she was female.

Years later, Stephanie said that she did not remember me telling her, but for me it was massive. I went through palpitations ahead of my planned disclosure. It was new territory for me: I had never shared this secret with anyone. In the end I fumbled out a miserable 'I've something to tell you – I have a thing about women's clothes.' My recollection of her reply is hazy and we rapidly changed the subject. However, the revelation was never for Stephanie's benefit – I had said what I thought I needed to say to clear my conscience before we built our future together, and that was it. There was never any discussion.

This was a burden I felt I could carry. I'd managed for as long as I could remember and, in any case, there was no alternative. By the 1990s, transsexuals may have gone to London rather than Casablanca for the surgeries that turned magic into reality, but it was totally beyond my experience. Meanwhile the activities advertised by transvestite groups – weekends away with other 'girls' – left me cold. They looked sordid and distasteful. Besides, it wasn't women's clothes that captivated me: I wanted a female body.

But I was no longer a five-year-old boy. I was now grown up and I was a scientist. The rational part of my brain took over – I worked hard to convince myself that since it was not possible to be a woman, there was no point thinking about it. My emotional side grieved all the same, but I had that beach ball under control. It was submerged and out of sight. Meanwhile there was a marriage to plan, a thesis to write and a career to start.

Stephanie and I married in the summer of 1993. We planned it ourselves in the church we attended weekly. Practical to the core, we spent the evening before with our friends in the church hall setting out tables and filling balloons with helium. On the morning of our wedding, I picked up the bread for the buffet while Stephanie got ready. Her brother drove her in the car that we had rented. We were twenty-five and twenty-three and we looked forward to a future together, hopefully with children. That boy who didn't want a relationship with a girl had grown into a man who now had a wife. I was pleased with how life had turned out; without the internet, it might well have continued that way.

There were occasional crises. Soon after we returned from our honeymoon, news filtered through to me about a friend of a friend. According to reports, he was now a she. Life was different for transitioners in the early 1990s, ten years before the Gender Recognition Act (GRA) and almost twenty before the Equality Act. There was no wave of affirmation, not that I could see anyway. Instead, gossip was shared in hushed whispers.

I wanted to know everything but learned almost nothing. However, for the first time in my life, it dawned on me that it was possible for people I knew – people like me, indeed – to transition. I was taken aback by how strongly the feelings hit me. Was I jealous? The discomfort I had been struggling with all my life suddenly became intense. Something I had long wanted to do became something I felt I needed to do.

But the problem stared me in the face – I had not the first clue how to do it. It was 1994; the internet was primitive and social media was still unknown. If I wanted to talk to someone, the discussion would need to happen in real life. Eventually, after several weeks agonising over it, I decided to seek advice from a member of the pastoral team at church.

He listened to what was only the second disclosure that I had ever made. This was a very different experience from that of telling Stephanie. We discussed my secret cross-dressing. At the time, it was something in the past, but experience told me that I would be unlikely to keep it at bay much longer. The conversation went on for maybe an hour. We covered transsexualism – 'an extreme response', we decided, and transvestism. We agreed that neither was something that men should be doing. Was that conversion therapy? However that meeting might be described three decades later, it was what I needed at the time. I cycled home to Stephanie. She was the person I wanted, not the fantasy in my head. The beach ball stayed down.

Life moved on. We both trained as teachers. Shortly afterwards – in 1997 – our daughter was born; she was followed by two sons, in 2000 and 2002. We had become a family of five and we were busy. At the same time, I was in the early years of a career in teaching. My days at school were long and they were filled with work. I would come home tired, eat, and then spend yet more time in the evening planning and marking.

But no matter how busy I was on the outside, my inner struggle always returned. Sometimes it was spontaneous;

other times it was precipitated by television programmes or newspaper pieces. Transsexuals may have been pitied, but they were hardly treated kindly. Prurient documentaries revealed the lives of transitioners and sometimes their partners, while tabloid headlines rang out the warnings to those in employment. 'Sex-Swap Teacher's Sordid Secret EXPOSED!' typified the narrative. Before the Equality Act, transsexuals were fair game. This really was something best avoided.

I was again buying women's clothes, and this time in the city where I worked. It was risky, but I no longer had the luxury of time that I had known as a fifteen-year-old. Once I feared that I had been rumbled. As I handed over my money, I saw a child in the corner of my eye. He looked like one of my pupils. With the sale completed, I had a good look. But he was gone. What to do now?

I went into school in trepidation. I had a job to do and I was determined to keep myself busy, but every glance, every whisper and every snigger – and schools are full of those – sent me into palpitations. I was convinced that news had spread like wildfire, and the children were gossiping about me. If I had been able to share my concerns with anyone, no doubt I would have been reassured that the pupils had far more interest in their own lives than in mine. And even if I had been spotted, the obvious conclusion would have been that I was on an errand, or maybe buying a present. If I had been in good mental health, then maybe I would have worked it out for myself. But I only relaxed when I moved on to another school in another city.

All was well on the outside, but on the inside those crav-
ings to change sex never went away. Information was increasingly available. No longer did I need to sit alone among the
books in the city library – the internet brought it into my
home. But we were still on dial-up. We connected once a
day to send the emails in our outbox, and then pick up the
incoming messages from the server. It was primitive and it
was slow. In the year 2000, a single photograph could hold
things up for what felt like hours. But alongside email, there
was the Web, and that gave me a glimpse of message boards
and forums. I spotted a community out there – one where
people transitioned and shared their experiences. I longed
to join them but – since my time online was so limited – I
could only watch, and then only for a few minutes at a time.

I was miserable. It seemed to me that I had the worst of
both worlds. I was aware of what was happening but unable
to join in. I knew I had to choose between finding out more –
spending more time online and maybe even joining one of
those forums – or going cold turkey. It was a dilemma: I
wanted to do the former, but we had a young family. With a
wife and children, I knew I needed to do the latter. Another
bag of clothes went to the tip, and I resolved to stay away
from those message boards and forums. So far, so good, but
I understood myself all too well. I had history, and I gave
myself six months. At most.

So, six years on from the second disclosure, I went looking
for help. As on the previous occasion, I confided in a male
friend. His response surprised me. He had come across
this before – once again I wondered how common this was

and not just in distant corners of the internet. I knew what I wanted from him, and I took the lead. I told him that I needed to be accountable, and I asked him to challenge me regularly about what I was buying, and what I was reading on the internet. He was happy to help and offered to have a quiet word at regular intervals.

Initially, it was a great success. I kept myself on the straight and narrow; when he challenged me, I answered truthfully. But six months was optimistic. Soon, I started making excuses not to see him or, when we did meet, I would make sure that it was in a larger group. When I anticipated that he was going to do what I had asked him to do, I would avoid eye contact and move the conversation on. I didn't tell lies; instead, I avoided the issue. I think he got the message, and he stopped trying to ask.

As the decade progressed, I made the dilemma work. Clothes were bought but then hidden away. Just knowing I had them was enough: I didn't need to actually wear them. In fact, they were secreted so well that it was more trouble than it was worth to dig them out. Besides, I knew that they suited me far better in my mind's eye than in reality. I was no longer a fifteen-year-old boy: I was a man in my thirties. I was tall and broad-shouldered, and I was hairy in the wrong places. The undeniable truth was that I did not suit the clothes that I was buying. They were not designed for me – they were designed for women.

The internet was accessible, but we kept the dial-up so for most of the day it was disconnected. While I made regular ventures online, I never communicated with anyone. I was there to seek information, not share it. For the time being at least, I was an observer rather than a participant. I knew far more about transition than I could ever have discovered in the library books of my youth, but it remained an academic interest. The subjects were other people, not me.

In 2008 I reached my fortieth birthday, and I congratulated myself on completing the first half of my life without caving in to my inner demons. Surely, now, I would also be able to manage the second. By then I had read enough about gender transition to know that people like me transitioned. Part of me grieved for what I had not been able to do, but I was also happy with my life. Our children were growing up, and I was successful in my teaching career. I was a head of department and I had significant responsibilities across the school. Stephanie had returned to work, so we both had jobs. We were content, and we were comfortable. Why would I want to upset something that was going so well?

2

TRANS ORTHODOXY

WHEN I entered my fifth decade, everything changed. Broadband had already replaced dial-up and, increasingly, the virtual world followed me around as I navigated the real one. But – more significantly – communication became a two-way affair. No longer was I merely a consumer of information posted by others: I could now ask questions of my own. It all felt deliciously anonymous. Throwaway profiles could be created in an instant and – if a conversation became uncomfortable – deleted the same day.

In many ways, searching the internet of 2010 for information on what were increasingly referred to as 'transgender issues' was like stepping out into the Wild West. Terms like 'transsexual' and certainly 'transvestite' were discouraged, but people don't change. Forums for transitioners were one click away from highly sexualised websites that peddled transvestite porn. Sometimes the line between the two groups blurred, but the sense of hierarchy was palpable. Transitioners would claim to be different from mere cross-dressers, and by 'different' it was clear that they meant 'better'. I knew which group I identified with. We – and these forums were almost exclusively the domain of male transitioners and wannabes – were 'trans women', always written with a space. We told ourselves that we were a type of woman because we had the same gender identity as 'other' women.

On those forums I asked my questions, and established users deluged me with answers. I immersed myself in this community and lapped up the groupthink. No longer did I yearn to be the opposite sex: I thought I really was the opposite sex – though 'gender' was the preferred word. According to the orthodoxy, I had suffered the misfortune of being born in the wrong body with the wrong genitals. I was told that studies had shown that we had brain patterns typical of our 'true gender' – new terminology that I lapped up eagerly. Explanations were offered. I heard that boys' brains were differentiated from girls' brains by hormone levels *in utero*. It seemed that men and women were not distinguished by the appearance of their genitals at birth, but by the level of sex hormones in their developing brains at critical periods before they were born.

As a scientist I should have challenged those claims. Even if all this was true – and I really had been deprived of testosterone *in utero* – how would that make me a woman? Similar theories were postulated for homosexuality. Gay men, I was told, were gay because they had been low in testosterone a couple of weeks before we were, or maybe it was a couple of weeks later? But gay men are not women because they are attracted to men, so why should trans women be women because they want to be women? Why were we not another unusual group of men?

But to challenge this orthodoxy I would have needed to stand apart from the group, and this was a group that re-assured me that there was nothing wrong with me psycho-logically. They were of one mind: my genitals were a mistake, and I was a woman like other women. It was other people who were the problem: it was they who needed to change their thinking and move beyond 'biological essentialism'. According to the groupthink, 'trans women were women', and anyone who thought differently was a bigot.

It might have been fantastic nonsense but it was the mes-sage I wanted to hear. If ideas could be savoured, this one tasted delicious. I was hooked. It was not for me to address a psychological disorder; instead the rest of society needed to affirm my true gender, and respect my gender identity. All I needed to do now was to 'come out'. But I had still told only three people in the real world, and I was no longer in touch with two of them. Only Stephanie remained and she was totally unaware of the ruminations going on in my mind.

In my head, I told myself that I needed to be my true self – a woman, or so I thought – but how could that tally with my role as husband and father of three? At that point, the orthodoxy failed me. There seemed to be no way to hold the inner and outer worlds together, and my mental health plummeted. Much as I wanted to 'snap out of it' – language I might have been guilty of using in my head, if not out loud, in my earlier years – I couldn't. My anxiety levels soared, and I became increasingly withdrawn. I spent more and more time on the internet, following other people's transitions – if they could do it, why not me? – and discussing my own plans for transition. At that point, it was still pure fantasy and no more tangible than my childhood daydreams. But I rapidly became captive to the concept of 'gender identity' – I believed that it made me a woman. I was also convinced that I would have to decide between transition or an endless deterioration in my mental health.

Gender identity is in fact a relatively new idea. The term was coined in 1964 by UCLA psychiatrists Robert Stoller and Ralph Greenson to describe the awareness 'I am a male' or 'I am a female'.[1] Meanwhile sex researcher John Money popularised the term 'gender role'.[2] Money became infamous for his now-notorious twins study.[3] On his advice, Bruce Reimer – a baby boy born in 1965– was transitioned to a girl following a botched circumcision that had destroyed his penis. Money believed that gender could be arbitrarily assigned to a child before the age of three and then reinforced with social messages – clothes, hairstyles and names. Bruce was renamed Brenda, and his twin brother acted as a control in what was a highly unethical experiment. Despite Money's claims to the contrary, the experiment was a disaster and, after learning the truth, Reimer refused to continue living as a girl when he was fourteen. But the impact on those children must have been monumental. Tragically, both twins took their own lives in their thirties.

Money was an advocate of gender reassignment surgery for patients dissatisfied with their gender, but it was Harry

Benjamin who gave his name to the condition. Benjamin – a German émigré – had established a medical practice in New York in 1915. Originally devoted to treatments to reverse the ageing process, he saw his first transsexual patient in 1948.[4] Unconvinced that psychotherapy would be effective, Benjamin recommended gender reassignment surgery. 'Harry Benjamin syndrome' was for a while synonymous with transsexualism, and in 1979 the Harry Benjamin International Gender Dysphoria Association (HBIGDA) issued the original Standards of Care for Gender Identity Disorders (SOC).[5] In 2006, HBIGDA became WPATH – the World Professional Association for Transgender Health.

But whatever might have been going on in the minds of Benjamin's patients, psychology is not biology and gender identity is not sex. However, in more recent times gender identity has been used to divide humanity in a way that was formerly the preserve of sex. In doing so, it extended its reach. The key question that I never asked was: does gender identity merely describe us, or does it define us? Does it simply label cross-sex behaviour, or is it an innate quality that trumps biological sex?

Legislators across the world have enshrined gender identity into law and policy, but appeals to authority offer poor support to arguments. What if the authorities are wrong? Definitions of gender identity tend to draw their inspiration from the introduction to the 'Yogyakarta Principles' of 2006:

> Gender identity is understood to refer to each person's
> deeply felt internal and individual experience of gender,

which may or may not correspond with the sex assigned at birth, including the personal sense of the body (which may involve, if freely chosen, modification of bodily appearance or function by medical, surgical or other means) and other expressions of gender, including dress, speech and mannerisms.[6]

The location – Yogyakarta, Indonesia – might have been exotic, and the conference might have comprised 'a distinguished group of human rights experts', but this was a meeting of minds with a clear agenda. They wanted to redefine one of the fundamental concepts in human society: the distinction between men and women. After Yogyakarta, gender identity was sold to the United Nations, to the Council of Europe, and to governments and administrations across the world.[7] In 2016, the idea would reach Westminster. When Maria Miller MP – chair of the House of Commons Women and Equalities Committee – urged the UK Parliament to enshrine gender identity as a protected characteristic in the UK Equality Act (displacing gender reassignment), she cited Yogyakarta: 'The current wording is outdated and confusing, and we believe that our proposed change would be in line with the Yogyakarta principles.'[8]

But for me, this was far more than a political debate, and it cut through to my core. I diagnosed myself with transsexualism and pored over the Standards of Care. The message I wanted to see was there in black and white: 'Psychotherapy is not intended to cure the gender identity disorder.'[9]

But at some point I had to get real. As my inner world spiralled, I finally let that beach ball come to the surface: I told Stephanie that something was wrong. It was the spring of 2011. Articulating those feelings was terrifying, but it was also liberating. The rush was addictive and, much to Stephanie's distress, I also told others. She feared losing control of the situation before we had had chance to explore the issues together. She was right; I was wrong. But I needed people to know what I thought was the real me. I wanted to be whole, and that meant bringing together the internal and external worlds. In truth, however, I only wanted one world to move, and it was not the fantasy that I had built inside my head.

The disconnect between what I believed and what everyone else could see was profound, and I had no evidence to back up my claims. Real life was somewhat different from internet chatrooms. 'I believe that I am really a woman,' I would declare to real-life friends, craving the same affirmation that I received from those disembodied voices online. The simplest of questions – 'Why do you think that?' – would leave me thrashing around with no coherent explanations. Any challenge – and that was how I viewed those questions – left me unable to cope. I would flee the room rather than face up to reality.

I believed that I was a woman, but that was not enough. I needed other people to believe it as well. Not only that, I needed to believe that they really did believe it, and were not just fobbing me off. It was no way to live, but it was all I had. Not surprisingly, I became more and more mentally unwell. Not that I saw it that way – as far as I was concerned there was nothing wrong with me – the problem was everyone else.

In my mind I was a woman because I had a female gender identity. When that was not immediately affirmed, it exacerbated what a psychiatrist would later diagnose as gender dysphoria. The rapid deterioration in my mental health fuelled my belief that I was indeed transsexual. The cycle was vicious: I began to chase my misery to confirm those beliefs. The worse I felt about myself, the more convinced I became that I needed to transition to feel better again.

I retreated to online forums. There, I found the unquestioning affirmation that I craved. But I became increasingly distant from Stephanie and the real world. I might have been there physically but mentally I was in another world. Two narratives tore through me like a pincer movement. The transition stories were a carrot. I was transfixed. People like me – engineers, medics, teachers – were becoming their true selves, or so they assured me. Yes, there were problems. But they could be managed. Before-and-after photos showed the magic of gender transition, and if they could do it, then so could I. Transition became an imperative. There was no shortage of online advice, so ignorance could no longer hold me back. I was jealous and desperate to follow. Meanwhile there was the stick. Dark stories were shared about others who had not transitioned and become increasingly dysfunctional, or worse. The message was clear, if not always articulated so bluntly: transition or die.

But reading about other people's transitions – or even mentally planning my own – was not the same as actually going through it, and turning my life upside down. And not only my life. I may have been self-absorbed but I could still recognise the likely impact on Stephanie and the children. Back on the forums I had been counselled that when a transsexual transitions, their family transitions with them – but doesn't reap the benefits. Such glib advice was pathetically inadequate, but I clung on to the idea that, despite everything, my family would come through this with me.

Transition became an all-consuming project. I saw a counsellor regularly, but it was therapeutic – or so I thought – just to tell people. To be fair, my employer did need to know – my work was undoubtedly affected by my poor mental health – but I enjoyed a rush of gender euphoria every time I came out to someone. I told the headteacher and his deputies. This was all becoming real, and it was exciting, for me at least. I wanted to rush ahead, but Stephanie urged caution. Perhaps I slowed down slightly? But I was still moving ten times faster than she would have wanted. During that very chaotic time in my life, even as I grew out my hair, we did not tell the children. They were totally unaware of my Wednesday-afternoon counselling sessions. As I explored my inner world, Stephanie held the family together.

One Wednesday, my counsellor put a chair in an open doorway. We had been going round in circles – on a roundabout, she suggested – and we needed to check out all the exits. The doorway, she said, was transition. While the chair blocked that path, we explored the other exits. At her insistence, we discussed living with dysphoria or perhaps finding some other outlet for it. She suggested *Second Life*, an online world where avatars could be created as either sex. I was dismissive. And nor was I interested in attending occasional cross-dressing weekends. My distress intensified and, rapidly, my ire was directed at that chair. I hated it. That inanimate object was stopping me doing what I wanted to do. It was still there during the next session, but I had had enough. I got up, walked across the room and moved the chair myself.

On that afternoon in July 2011, I decided that there really was no alternative to transition. This was something that was going to happen. The counsellor affirmed my decision – I was paying her after all. But affirmative psychotherapy – if that isn't a contradiction – was not enough: I needed to talk to someone who had been through it themselves, to find out for real. We met in a coffee bar in an arts centre in August. Our backgrounds were similar – we were both teachers and both churchgoers – and we had been corresponding online for several weeks. My friend was convalescing from gender reassignment surgery and needed to sit on a 'doughnut cushion'. I had read about such paraphernalia, but now it was real. As was the advice – transition if you must but it will probably wreck your career and almost certainly destroy your marriage. But driving home afterwards, I ruminated on something else. As we paid for our drinks, the waitress thanked us. She called us 'sir and madam'. I was the sir, and I hated myself for it.

Three weeks later my GP prescribed propranolol – an anti-anxiety drug – to calm me down. Two weeks later he directed me to a community psychiatrist. Four weeks after that, the psychiatrist referred me to the NHS Gender Identity Clinic (GIC) in London. Locally, I paid for a course of facial-hair removal. Meanwhile, my employer brought in a consultant to advise on transition at work – so at least my career seemed safe. But at home Stephanie managed as best as she could.

The GIC saw me in May 2012. Going straight from work, I attended the appointment dressed in suit and tie. At that time the clinic was based in offices above a shop in Hammersmith, a hundred metres from Charing Cross Hospital. I pressed the bell and spoke into a grille. The receptionist released the heavy brown door and I made my way tentatively up the stairs. Confusingly perhaps, the GIC was also known as 'Charing Cross', but it was administered by a different NHS trust, and no longer part of the hospital. The psychiatrist took down my history; I asked about hormone therapy. The clinician looked at me and asked me when I was going to transition – 'full-time', she added. Despite my secretive cross-dressing activities over the years, I had never been out of the house in women's clothes. I knew I had much to learn, but my transition plan was all set out in meticulous detail. 'December 20th,' I replied.

'Come back in February,' she said. 'We can discuss hormones then.'

However critical I might have been of the GIC, at least I was getting support; there was no help for Stephanie. We arranged a time to tell our children, and then our families. They were shocked, hurt and upset. They did not share my sense of liberation; for them there were no benefits, but complications, difficulties and a sense of loss. Then, on the last day of the autumn term – the winter solstice – my pupils went home for Christmas and I became Debbie for all purposes.

Life went on. When anyone asked me, I explained that my aim was to keep my job and stay out of the press. After a nervous couple of days at the start of the spring term, school settled down. Lessons were taught and books were marked, much as before. Some things maybe even changed for the better. Van de Graaff generator demonstrations were so much better now that my hair was below my shoulders, and the cheap jewellery I had bought was excellent for demonstrating magnetic and non-magnetic metals. Most of mine was magnetic, and therefore steel rather than silver. Other lessons, however, were trickier to teach, especially when I wore a skirt. I refrained from jumping down from the bench to demonstrate the physics of free fall. But no journalist took any interest, if they even heard about me. Beyond my own family, nobody seemed to care.

There was novelty in changing my name in various places, but that soon became a chore. Family life returned to a new normal. I was still Dad, and – at my children's request – *he/him* at home. That was one detail I chose not to share with the GIC.

At my second appointment in February 2013, I dressed in a skirt and went armed with a bundle of papers – including my change-of-name document, and a reference from my employer. The clinic seemed happy enough with my progress, and another psychiatrist recommended hormones. The following year – March 2014 – I was referred for gender reassignment surgery. That should have happened within eighteen weeks, but waiting lists were beginning to grow and I languished in a long and slow-moving queue until February

2016. Meanwhile the GIC saw me every six months or so, but there was little to talk about. I recounted anecdotes from school; they wrote them down and put them in the file.

Whatever benefits I had expected from social transition and hormone therapy, they were not enough. I convinced myself that I needed surgery. As the eighteen weeks became six months, and then a year, I struggled. Then, people who had been referred after me got to the operating theatre before I did. Much depended on where the referral had been sent. Three hospitals offered gender reassignment surgery, so there were three separate queues. After choosing our lane we were stuck with it, and I was clearly in the slowest one. My frustration grew; I called it acute gender dysphoria. But how different was it from the feelings of annoyance when the other lines move faster at the post office, or anger when someone nips up the outside lane and then cuts in before the road narrows? Whatever language we use, human emotions are much the same. I wanted surgery, and I became irritated that I had to wait longer than others.

But in all other respects, my transition was going well. I had chosen a good window in time. The NHS had just ended a so-called 'postcode lottery' for gender reassignment surgery. Previously, some Primary Care Trusts funded it, while others saw it as a cosmetic procedure that patients could pay for themselves. Meanwhile, the still-recent Equality Act 2010 included gender reassignment as one of nine protected characteristics – according to the law, it was unlawful to treat me 'less favourably' just because I had transitioned. But I lived and worked in liberal and accepting communities and, from most people, the support was genuine and not merely compliant with the law.

My confidence grew, as did my competence with clothes and make-up. My goal was to pass as a woman, and not be clocked as trans. Of course, I could never be sure if others were just being kind but – in the main – nobody seemed to notice. Early in transition I checked these things by asking a friend to walk twenty paces behind me and count the second glances. They were few and far between. No wonder: other people had their own lives to live – why should they care about me? I thought of myself as a woman – albeit 'with a trans history' – and I assumed the right to use women's spaces and take up their places. In my mind, I had transitioned and that was the end of the matter.

After a couple of years, I began to develop new interests. Politics had always run in my blood but, when it came to campaigning, I was a mere foot soldier. Others addressed meetings; I delivered leaflets. I was also an active member of the teaching union the NASUWT. By 2015 I had been a workplace representative for over a decade, but I was content to follow policy that others had developed. News about conferences and national campaign strategies filtered through to me via articles in the union magazine, but invitations and opportunities went no further than the recycling bin. That all changed in February 2015. Nicky Morgan MP – the secretary of state for education at the time – was an advertised speaker at the forthcoming NASUWT conference for LGBT members. I signed up. I wanted to hear what she had to say.

Alas, I never found out. Morgan sent apologies at the last minute. But I was there, and I heard what others had to say. Trans people were a small minority at the conference, and there was a plea for one of us perhaps to join the union's national LGBT committee. I pushed at that door and it opened; it was the first of many. Nine months later – in November 2015 – I joined the national TUC LGBT+ committee that met at Congress House in London. The Trades Union Congress brings together 48 affiliated unions, including the NASUWT. Committee places had been reserved for trans people from any of those unions but few came forward to fill them. That year two candidates filled two places. The following year, I was elected alongside a vacancy. The committee work was straightforward. We were elected by the annual TUC LGBT+ workers' conference, and we convened five times a year. The committee received reports from TUC officials, and we oversaw the planning of the next conference.

The focus of our work was TUC policy and procedures that had an impact on LGBT workers. But the politics of the trade union movement were ever present. The learning curve was steep. I had been nominated by the NASUWT, and I represented the interests of my own union and reported back to NASUWT officials. The networking around meetings brought me into contact with senior officials, general secretaries and politicians. Doors were standing wide open before I even got to them.

When I first joined the TUC LGBT+ committee, the work seemed to be at a crossroads, or perhaps on one of my counsellor's roundabouts. The key battles had already been won for same-sex attracted people. Section 28 had been repealed, gay and lesbian people could serve in the military, the age of consent had been equalised, and same-sex marriage was on the statute books. What more was there to do? Unsympathetic employers continued to generate casework, but while that ongoing toil was bread-and-butter work for trade unionists, it was hardly going to change society or satisfy the appetites of political campaigners. There was interest – quite rightly – in the repression faced by LGBT workers in other parts of the world, while one committee colleague pushed tirelessly for the TUC to take an interest in the NHS blood-transfusion service. At the time, men who had sex with other men were prohibited from giving blood even if they were in a stable, exclusive relationship. But these campaigns were marginal at best. Something new was needed, and it was clear that that something was trans.

The message I heard seemed to me to have been well rehearsed, and it was one I felt I was expected to share: life was grim for trans people. That was certainly not my experience, however. I was successful at work and, now I had been released from the classroom to attend committee meetings in London, my professional life had become much more varied and interesting. When dreadful anecdotes were reported to the committee, I always wondered what was really going on. Life can be difficult for everyone. It was never clear whether the tales of discrimination, harassment and abuse had arisen because the victims were trans, or because of something else. I sometimes suspected the latter, but I was new to the committee and kept those ideas to myself.

There was no doubt, however, that the focus was shifting away from LGB to the T. But the two groups were not the same, and nor were their demands. Lesbian and gay people had not campaigned to impose themselves on others, and nor did they display the egregious sense of entitlement that I perceived from some trans campaigners. By 2015, the campaign for trans equality – whatever that meant – was already having an impact on the rights of women. At lunchtime during my very first committee meeting we discussed an online petition that called on Cardiff University to cancel a proposed lecture by Germaine Greer. Greer, the petitioners argued, had 'demonstrated misogynistic views towards trans women, including continually misgendering trans women and denying the existence of transphobia altogether'.[10] As the only trans person in the room, my views were eagerly sought.

I was unimpressed by the petitioners – if they were so confident that Greer was wrong why couldn't they ask her some difficult questions and prove that she was wrong? – and I was unhappy that trans people were being used to try to silence a well-known campaigner. But at the same time I was troubled by Greer's language. Responding to the furore, she had declared: 'What they are saying is that because I don't think surgery will turn a man into a woman I should not be allowed to speak anywhere.'[11]

I had transitioned because I thought I was a woman – just one who had had the misfortune to have been born in the wrong body. Who was Greer to tell me that I was not?! At the time I was awaiting the surgery that would confirm it.

So I was guarded in my response as I ate my lunch: 'It's a difficult issue and we need to think about it carefully.'

Back in 2015, my thinking was orthodox – 'trans women are women', and if some people didn't like it then they needed to 'get over it'. I never wore that slogan on a T-shirt, but I was still trying to build my life on that philosophy. In my mind I was a woman, and I assumed that that impression was replicated in everyone else's mind. I never tried to control anyone else's speech, let alone their thoughts, but I never felt I needed to. After three years of so-called 'living as a woman', I had become adept at creating the illusion. I certainly didn't need to announce my pronouns: others used them habitually. If a visitor to the school wanted to find me, for example, colleagues might say: 'If you're looking for Debbie, she is a tall woman with grey hair. You can probably find her in the staffroom.' It would have made no sense for anyone to say anything else. If it looked like a duck, waddled like a duck and quacked like a duck, then it was a duck. In the same way I was a woman.

By that time, changing names and markers from male to female was a task long since completed – almost. My passport, driving licence and most other documents all declared me to be female. There were, however, three exceptions. I gave up trying to explain the concept of gender change to the overseas call centre operated by my telecoms provider. Since they sent the bills to Dr D. Hayton, that hardly seemed an issue. I never bothered with the Land Registry – they did not send me letters, ever. But significantly, I never applied for a Gender Recognition Certificate (GRC) to change my legal sex.

According to the Gender Recognition Act 2004, I would have been eligible to apply for a GRC from December 2014. And thanks to the passing of the Marriage (Same Sex Couples) Act 2013, Stephanie and I would not have needed to divorce as part of the deal. Previously, couples would divorce and – if they so wished – establish a civil partnership in place of their marriage. A fast-track system, I was told, allowed both processes to take place on the same day. But, even so, we had been married in a church, in a Christian ceremony. Equal marriage did not extend to the Church, so we would need to swap our Church marriage for a civil alternative. Not only would I get a new birth certificate, one that declared me to have been born a girl, we would need to exchange our marriage certificate for one that said we had been married in a register office. That second legal fiction was a step too far. Besides, there seemed no need to lie about the past to live in the present. How often is one required to produce a birth certificate in any case?

I was a woman – that was what I told myself. I might have had a trans history – maybe even a male history – but it was the future that I was bothered about. Gender reassignment surgery was just around the corner. Then seeing really would be believing. Or would it? The beach ball was long gone but deep down there was a tiny piece of grit in the oyster. I couldn't see it – I didn't want to see it – but I could feel it. I knew that Germaine Greer did not think I was a woman. Neither did some other writers whom I respected. Julie Bindel had once been characteristically down to earth in *The Guardian*, of all places. She wrote: 'I don't have a problem with men disposing of their genitals, but it does not make them women, in the same way that shoving a bit of vacuum hose down your 501s does not make you a man.'[12]

How many other women – and men – did not believe my assertion of womanhood? I did not know and – because I did not know – I could never experience the peace and contentment that I coveted. But I could not dwell on the thoughts of others, or the illusion may have collapsed. Besides, my transition project still filled up my time. There was a clinic appointment with the specialist nurse to tick off, a long absence from work to plan, and then the surgery itself. I kept my eye on the prize and dismissed the doubts, worries and concerns. I had waited a long time for GRS, and I was determined to go through with it.

3

AWAKENING

I N the end I was lucky. Prolapses can and do happen after GRS; incontinence is a thing, and permanent numbness is all too common. But my problems were transitory. With the blockages and infections behind me, the carpentry held up, the plumbing worked and – as for the electrics – sensation returned after about six months. I took it easy in the weeks after surgery; I had no alternative. Sitting was painful – though I never succumbed to a doughnut cushion – and my days were punctuated by dilations. Three times every day I would go through the ritual: preparation; five minutes with the 25-mm dilator, then twenty with the 30-mm; shower and clear up. After ninety minutes, I was free to go.

Nine weeks after surgery, the dilations reduced from three to two – morning and evening. Two weeks later I returned to work, and life returned with a vengeance. Suddenly there were lessons to plan, books to mark and reports to write. At the same time, I prepared to speak at a Westminster Social

Policy Forum seminar.[1] The date was 15 June 2016, and the theme was 'policy priorities for transgender equality'. It was already a hot topic in politics – back in January, the House of Commons Women and Equalities Committee had published a ninety-seven-page report devoted to the issue.[2] A member of that committee – Labour MP Ruth Cadbury – was chairing part of the seminar; as a trans member of the TUC LGBT+ committee, I had been invited to join a panel to talk about transgender rights in employment.

As a trade union officer, I talked about trade union issues: cases of discrimination, harassment and unfair treatment that trans people had suffered. Whatever else might be said about us, trans people are indeed people, and it is not therefore surprising that we can also suffer poor experiences in the workplace. Whether they are worse or more numerous is harder to know, but thankfully I was not pushed on that or anything else. The audience was remarkably generous to me, and I might have returned home affirmed but uneducated had it not been for two interruptions – neither of which was in the organisers' script.

Dr Julia Long – a lecturer at Anglia Ruskin University – spoke from the floor. She directed her remarks to Ruth Cadbury: 'My question also relates to the term "gender identity". I think you know a lot of feminists, whose voices weren't listened to by your committee, pointed out the serious flaws in this concept of gender identity, which as far as I can see is undefined in the report.'

As Long continued, she highlighted the 'very serious implications for women and women's safety' if anyone could claim to be a different sex on the basis of self-declaration. The anxiety that enveloped the room was palpable. Inside my head, I felt the discomfort personally. What indeed *is* gender identity, I pondered. It was a question I had never been asked and it was something I had never much thought about. In June 2016, gender identity was something I still took for granted. Exactly four months earlier, I had told the anaesthetist to 'go for it' because I believed that I had a female gender identity. Now, for the first time, I searched my head for proof of that gender identity; I found nothing.

The second interjection was private. After sitting down from speaking, I glanced around the room. What had the audience made of what I said, I wondered. I flicked through Twitter in an attempt to find out. A cryptic tweet caught my eye: '#Transgender policy? Listen to parents #FirstDoNoHarm #silencednomore'.[3]

My Twitter handle was tagged in with four others. To my mind, that message screamed out for a response but none was forthcoming. The meeting ended, pleasantries were shared, and I went home to Birmingham. As the train travelled north my thoughts ruminated on Long's remarks and that tweet. At 5.08 p.m., I responded: 'The more listening we do, the better.'[4]

Half an hour later, my unknown interlocutor replied: 'Yes, listen to parents,' adding links to two blog pieces, before finishing the message with 'Talking about #teachers'.[5]

Social media changed my world for the second time. Five years after exposing me to communities of transgender people, it now brought me in contact with a different group of people, and a totally different way of thinking. The two pieces spoke not about women's rights but the impact of gender identity on children.

In one first-person account, a parent talked about her son who had been 'born twenty-four years ago into a body that was healthy, beautiful, strong and (potentially) fertile'. She spoke about his obsession with gender and his experience with an NHS 'gender specialist': 'Far from neutral, this "gender specialist" actively proselytizes for medical intervention, offering what my son regards as a "diagnosis of being trans" but which is in fact an echo of my son's internet-based self-diagnosis.'[6]

Her son – once a 'happy, healthy, academically successful and sociable young person' – was now a virtual recluse, sleeping most of the day and spending most of the night playing computer games on the internet. It was heartbreaking. What could I say? I replied as best I could: 'Thank you for sharing the articles. I've read them both.'[7]

That was the first of four bombshells that changed my way of thinking in the summer of 2016. The second came just over a month later. It was a bright sunny morning in July, a perfect day for driving. Stephanie had been away for over a week on a silent retreat in Wales. I stayed at home to look after our sons, but, early that morning, I set out to pick her up. There was just me in the car – I had left before the teenagers surfaced – and the choice of listening was mine. As I drove out of Abergavenny, BBC Radio 4 was broadcasting an episode of *Bringing Up Britain*. The presenter and her guests were discussing parenting through questions of gender identity.[8] I slowed down to ensure that I did not arrive at the retreat centre before the end of the programme.

A male clinician on the panel suggested that 'most thirteen- and fourteen-year-olds probably have a good idea of who they are and what their gender identity consists of'. Two months earlier I would likely have cheered him on. But my views were changing fast. Gender identity had consequences and, in the lives of the young people I had been reading about, becoming a recluse was one negative outcome among many. He was challenged by a female panellist, Stephanie Davies-Arai, who 'disagreed completely'. She added:

> The teenage years are a time of searching for your identity. Teenagers used to be able to move through different identities, and they would reach the time when the teenage brain fully finishes its development and becomes mature in the mid-twenties. Teenagers are not known for their decision-making skills [and] they have no idea about future consequences.

What dreadful things were we doing to children? I pondered that question as I drove the last mile. Without gender identity – which I had never been able to define, even to myself – what was going on? I had transitioned because I thought I had a gender identity; without it, what had I done to myself? Realisation was dawning that I had done it without knowing why, and I was not a teenager – I was approaching fifty.

I had been left with big questions to answer, but by then Stephanie was in sight, and I packed those thoughts away for later. I had turned Stephanie's life – and our children's lives – upside down in my quest to be the woman on the outside that I thought I was on the inside. Now, less than six months after GRS, the certainty that I was some kind of woman eluded me. But I knew that I had some serious thinking to do before I said anything.

What had compelled my transition if it had not been a gender identity inconsistent with my sex? As I had understood it, gender identity was far more profound than mere description – the gender with which we might identify. Rather, it was a fundamental and innate quality – like a gendered soul, perhaps? But it was impossible to pin down. Realisation was dawning in my mind that gender identity explained nothing. Instead, it explained away the truth. I needed an explanation that made sense, and one that was supported by rather more than crude sexual stereotypes.

But without gender identity as a crutch, how else could I justify the surgery that I had consented to, so willingly and so recently? The compulsion had been real. If it had not been a response to gender, could it be rooted in my sexuality? It was another transsexual – Miranda Yardley – who first attempted to explain autogynephilia to me. Not that we got very far in our discussions, and so, for the time being at least, that third bombshell fizzled and went out. Elsewhere in trans society, autogynephilia was talked about in whispers and rejected as shameful. The literal definition – 'a male's propensity to be sexually aroused by the thought of himself as a female' – was everything that we convinced ourselves we were not.[9] We were 'trans women', with that space between the two words.

A type of woman, we would assert. We were not male, and we certainly did not fancy ourselves.

Yardley was one of several trans people I was messaging privately. Another of those interlocutors delivered the fourth bombshell, and this time in person. I never did find out Christina's surname; we only met once, and we lost touch shortly afterwards. But that discussion over lunch changed my life. As we munched our way through our pizzas, the conversation became profound. Christina's point was phrased as a question: 'You know them TERFs, Debbie?'

'TERF' was already a slur. Originally standing for 'trans-exclusionary radical feminist', it had become a derogatory term for anyone who was thought to be 'anti-trans'. The bar tended to be set very low.

Reject the concept of gender identity? TERF!

Look at a trans person for slightly too long? TERF!

Refuse to give way to a trans person in debate? TERF!

Men can be TERFs as well, but it is women who tend to suffer the consequences of the label. If they are the modern-day witches, then the internet is full of witchfinders-general, eager to take out their fury on women who have the audacity to think for themselves. It is a dreadful term and – even then – one I recoiled from. But at the same time, I wanted to know what Christina thought about those women. 'Go on,' I replied.

'I think they're right. Or at least 90 per cent right.'

The immediate context was that ninety-seven-page report from the Women and Equalities Committee. It concluded with several pages of recommendations for the government.

Some were uncontroversial – the committee called out long NHS waiting times, for example. But two key proposals were already seeding disquiet and discontent. On gender recognition, the committee was uncompromising:

> Within the current Parliament, the Government must bring forward proposals to update the Gender Recognition Act, in line with the principles of gender self-declaration that have been developed in other jurisdictions. In place of the present medicalised, quasi-judicial application process, an administrative process must be developed, centred on the wishes of the individual applicant, rather than on intensive analysis by doctors and lawyers.[10]

Not *should* or *could*; the committee was insistent – *must!* But allowing anyone to simply choose their gender – and, in effect, their legal sex – rendered women's boundaries meaningless. That was self-evident. Women would be unable to maintain their sex-based rights if anyone could be female. It was no wonder that women were protesting. Our perspective was different, but it was clear to both of us that self-declaration was a bad idea. Arguably, it was the perception that gender reassignment was an intensive process carried out by specialist doctors that underpinned the public's respect for the process. Take away the official gatekeeping, we reasoned, and women may well introduce informal gatekeeping of their own that may be far less welcoming of transsexuals.

But contrary to what the committee seemed to believe, gender recognition was hardly an intensive process. Two medical reports – paid for by the client – and a diagnosis of gender dysphoria, and Bob's your aunt. In fact, as I had found personally, nobody really needed to go to any of that trouble. I had never bothered to have my gender recognised, and I didn't seem to suffer as a result. My birth certificate still announced – correctly – that I had been born a boy, but how often does anyone want to see that? Whenever I was clocked as trans, and therefore male, the assumption that I must therefore have been through some sort of legal gatekeeping was sufficient. The illusion depended not on legal paperwork but on perception and assumption. It seemed remarkable to both of us that anyone would want to throw a spanner in the works.

The second concern was 'gender identity'. That undefinable term was clearly in the ascendancy. The committee wanted to open up the Equality Act. Their report asserted: 'it is clear to us that the use of the terms "gender reassignment" and "transsexual" in the Act is outdated and misleading.' That was certainly not clear to two transsexuals finishing off their pizza. Gender reassignment is a process, something that people *do*. It can be observed and documented, and it can therefore be protected objectively in law. The committee, however, had other ideas: 'The protected characteristic in respect of trans people under the Equality Act should be amended to that of "gender identity".'

The reasoning was so weak it was laughable. It seemed that the law would be improved because the language would be 'brought up to date', and made compliant with Council of Europe Resolution 2048 – which I learned had been debated and adopted by the Parliamentary Assembly in Strasbourg the previous year.[11] Instead, we saw meaningful protections being replaced by words and ideas that the committee could not even define. I grasped at straws. 'They can't really mean this, can they?'

'They can and they do,' Christina assured me, 'and this will not be the end of it.'

Before we parted company, Christina recommended two videos to me. I clicked on the first link as soon as I got home. I watched Dr Rebecca Reilly-Cooper slowly and carefully dismantle the concept of gender identity.[12] As a philosopher and an academic she pulled it apart until there was nothing left. Not only was it undefined, it became very clear that it could never be defined because we can never get inside other people's heads to compare our experiences. The definition they offered in Yogyakarta – 'each person's deeply felt internal and individual experience of gender' – was circular and relied on the sexist stereotypes of 'dress, speech and mannerisms', not because they were lazy but because they had nothing better.

As the video continued to play, my belief that I could be a woman because of feelings in my head was evaporating quickly. Two thirds of the way through her hour-long lecture, I pressed stop. Once again, I was on my counsellor's round-about and this time there were three exits.

Straight ahead of me, I could delete the video from my phone, and never think about any of this ever again. That was the easy route, the one that led me back to the place I had come from. It was well populated with those who lived their lives in blissful ignorance of Reilly-Cooper's arguments. But I wanted to hear her conclusion because I suspected she was right. Of course, I could have dismissed her argument as inconvenient, and held on to my gender identity as a helpful fiction – a model that didn't need to be literally true. That was the second exit, but it seemed to be an exercise in abandoning intellectual honesty. Or I could take the third exit and abandon gender identity altogether. That would take courage. I couldn't see far beyond the exit – the road took a sharp turn and after that I would be in unknown territory.

For twenty-four hours, my mind went round in circles. As I pondered my decision, I played the second video.[13] Christina had warned me that it was uncompromising. Magdalen Berns had been a physics student at Edinburgh University, but she was notable for her YouTube vlogs. While Reilly-Cooper had carefully undermined gender identity with intellectual arguments, Berns flattened it in three minutes. Her opening salvo prepared the ground: 'I still don't know what it means when someone says they live full-time as a transwoman, especially when they look like a bloke.'*

---

* 'Trans woman' or 'transwoman'? Space or no space? Within the transgender debate, phrases, words and even spaces can make a political statement. 'Trans woman' – with a space – tends to be preferred by those who believe that 'trans women are women'. 'Trans' becomes an adjective to specify a type of woman. Those who think differently, like me, may prefer the single compound word. As I understand the words, transwomen are not women, perhaps like seahorses are not horses, or ladybirds are not birds. In this book I have used both forms, depending on context. So, for example, in Magdalen Berns's speech, 'transwoman' is transcribed without a space – Berns was clear that she thought Alex Drummond was 'a bloke'. Drummond, on the other hand, self-identified as some kind of woman, a 'trans woman', with a space.

Her target was Alex Drummond, a member of the Stonewall Trans Advisory Group. Stonewall – the gay and lesbian charity founded in 1989 to campaign against the now-infamous Section 28 – had recently become 'trans-inclusive'.[14] The Trans Advisory Group was established to help shape the charity's work 'with, and for, trans communities'. Berns dissected a video featuring Drummond – a self-described 'trans woman' who sported a full beard, and saw it as a talking point. 'So you're curious about the beard, huh?'[15]

Berns was clinical in her response: 'It's quite normal for blokes to have beards.' Quite! When Drummond claimed to be expanding the bandwidth of what it means to be a woman, Berns asked why not 'widen the bandwidth of being male'? She dismissed Drummond's claim that fixing cars with a boiler suit on 'doesn't take away my femininity' with a curt 'It doesn't make you female either, Alex.'

This time there was no time to ponder. Berns concluded her brief presentation with an attack on Stonewall: 'Your minds are so open, your brains have fallen out.' Whatever lay beyond the sharp turn from the roundabout, the hazards on the easy exits now stared me in the face. My brain might not literally fall out, but unless I used it, the impact on my integrity would be much the same. After watching the remaining twenty minutes of Reilly-Cooper's lecture, I abandoned my faith in gender identity and took the third exit from the roundabout.

My progress was rapid. The territory might have been unknown but it was not unfamiliar. Around that bend was just another part of me. It was not my Christian faith that changed my way of thinking that summer, but reason and logic. The evidence was overwhelming. I was a male human being – a man, therefore – who preferred to be perceived as a woman. But it was a lonely journey for a trans person to take. As my thinking developed, the trans people with whom I had transitioned became more and more distant. But as long as I was just thinking, they did not seem to notice.

A House of Commons debate on 1 December 2016 prompted me to crystallise my new ideas in print. The focus was 'transgender equality'. Christina had been right – that ninety-seven-page report was not the end of it. The committee chair – Conservative MP Maria Miller – opened the debate. She called on the government to give 'unequivocal commitments' to change the Gender Recognition Act 2004, 'in line with the principles of gender self-declaration', and open up the Equality Act 2010 to create 'a new protected characteristic of gender identity'.[16]

This debate could not itself lead to a change in the law, but it prepared the ground for a government bill that may well have done. The juggernaut was in motion, and those with power and influence seemed just to cheer it on. Those who saw the dangers and called them out – Julia Long, Stephanie Davies-Arai, Miranda Yardley, to name but three – were either ignored or condemned for their so-called transphobia.

The blog piece I wrote ahead of that debate was gentle compared to some of my later writings: I merely urged caution and my focus was squarely on the rights of transsexuals. I concluded:

Protections may be weakened not strengthened if self-declaration replaces expert testimony, and gender identity replaces gender reassignment as a protected characteristic. We need to reflect on the reality of the society we live in before we rush into a world where facts are replaced by feelings and evidence is replaced by the ethereal. I have therefore asked my MP to oppose the motion, and I urge others to do likewise.[17]

I watched the debate; my MP didn't feature. For two hours, a succession of politicians seemed to outbid each other to become the biggest trans ally in Parliament. An intervention by Caroline Flint (Labour) was notable because she urged caution, specifically on gender-neutral toilets:

I welcome the debate, because it is vital for us to consider the issue of transgender rights, but should we not also be wary of creating gender-neutral environments that may prove more of a risk to women themselves?… How does the right honourable Lady [Maria Miller] think we can protect women from male violence in gender-neutral environments?

Miller's dismissive response sounded well prepared: 'An aeroplane does not have a men's and a ladies', and we do not see any significant problems on aeroplanes.' There was no room for dissent and no room for caution: trans people were the victims – 'among the most marginalised in society', according to Angela Crawley of the SNP – and politicians were eager to be the rescuers. But a 'Karpman drama triangle' – a social model of human interaction proposed in the 1960s by the psychiatrist Stephen B. Karpman – also needs a persecutor.[18] Ruth Cadbury complained about doctors – 'too often acting as gatekeepers, preventing people from even entering the transition pathway' – and the criminal justice system: 'with every news story that a transgender woman has been sent to a men's prison, our frustration grows further.'

As I followed the debate from home, my frustration bubbled over. How could a Member of Parliament be so naive? Sending self-declared 'transgender women' to women's prisons presented a massive safeguarding loophole, and one that would surely be noticed by every abusive man who was on the lookout for such weaknesses. Vulnerable women in prison would suffer dreadfully – they don't get to choose who they share their spaces with – and the inevitable fallout would damage the trust and confidence that transsexuals like me relied on.

It did not take long for abusers to take up the offer. The following year Karen White sexually assaulted two women while on remand at HMP New Hall – a women's prison. According to reports, White had been 'born male and now identifies as a woman', whatever that meant.[19] Speaking later to a journalist, one of White's victims said: 'Karen White faked being transgender to abuse women and the authorities enabled her to assault and prey on us.'[20]

Those MPs might have wanted to be kind, or at least to be seen to be kind, but it seemed to me that their brains had indeed fallen out. At stake was the legal distinction between men and women, a fundamental issue that needed to be discussed and debated. Instead, there was affirmation of and acquiescence to the assertion that gender identity alone was the key, and that trans people – with our supposed special knowledge about our gender identity – must not be challenged.

That apparently rigid adherence to what I have since called 'gender identity ideology' was mirrored in my own political arena. By the spring of 2017, the TUC LGBT+ committee was becoming increasingly concerned about transphobia in the press, and in particular in the *Morning Star*. The *Star* might be a niche left-wing publication, but it reports on trade union issues that other newspapers overlook. To the dismay of some committee members, the paper had also published some feature articles that had promoted biological reality and defended the sex-based rights of women. One piece concluded: 'If the transgender identity is so fragile that for validation it must coercively redefine what it is to be a woman and monopolise feminist debate, then it is the ideology that has to change, not women.'[21]

In the minds of some of my colleagues, the *Star* was a platform for transphobia. In reality, the paper was platforming a transsexual. That piece had been written by Miranda Yardley. But being trans was an insufficient defence against accusations of being 'anti-trans': what mattered were opinions, and specifically the right sort of opinions.

Other articles were penned by women. Rebecca Reilly-Cooper had already dismantled gender identity on video. Her piece for the *Star*, 'Redefining women: not an easy debate', argued that 'a shift towards a subjective and individual assessment of who is and isn't a woman based on self-identification could be open to abuse'.[22] Quite! Then, four days later, Jennifer Duncan explained 'why I won't accept the politics of gender identity'.[23]

Some committee members were aghast. If gender identity ideology was a religious cult, then the *Morning Star* had been printing blasphemy. Representations were made to the editor. If this was a trade union newspaper, the committee decided, then he should listen to trade unionists. During those negotiations he agreed to carry a 'trans-positive' piece. Who better to write it than a member of the TUC LGBT+ committee who was also trans? My journalistic career was born.

Published on 14 April 2017, that first piece – 'How to avoid trans stereotyping?' – was anodyne. I regretted the nature of the debate that I described as 'polarised and toxic'. In the opening paragraphs I suggested that 'suspicion and mistrust have taken root, playing into the hands of those who oppress both women and trans people alike'.[24] I was happy and the committee was happy, but my plea for everyone to play nicely together was hardly going to win over hearts and minds in what was already a febrile dispute between two world views: biological sex or gender identity? With something as fundamental as the distinction between men and women at stake, there could be no compromise.

Already I knew which side I stood on in that debate. Even if I was in a minority of one on the committee, I had become an unbeliever in gender identity ideology. For the time being I kept my counsel, but when Jeremy Corbyn – then leader of the Labour Party – announced his support for gender self-identification, I pitched my own piece to the *Star*.[25] This time I wrote in a personal capacity. While I argued that the law was 'in desperate need of reform', I was clear that 'we must not forget the rights of women'. I asked questions: 'should female facilities be open to anyone who declares themselves to be a woman, or should limits be set?' What about women-only shortlists? 'Should those positions be open to anyone who identifies as a woman irrespective of their socialisation and how they present in society?'[26]

When that piece was published on 21 July 2017, it was not just me who asked questions. While I equivocated in the piece, merely opening up a discussion was potential sedition in the trans community – and on the committee. I was on thin ice, and I knew it. But to move forwards there was no alternative.

The *Star* might have a limited circulation, but my writing – and my ideas – became known to other journalists and editors. If anyone wanted a trans voice to speak out against gender self-identification – 'self-ID', as it was becoming known – they knew where to come. In early November I was interviewed for *The Times*.[27] Again, I was more cautious in public than I was in private. I spoke about casual discrimination against trans people in the workplace – something close to my heart as a trade unionist – and pointed out that that was what I wanted to see tackled, not self-ID, which I described as 'a battle that is totally unnecessary'.

I was treated with dignity and respect by the journalist and the newspaper. My interview was written up, and I approved the final copy before publication on 6 November 2017. Early that morning, I rushed to the newsagent; I was delighted with what I saw in print. There were three interviews in a balanced piece. Opening up was Miranda Yardley; I came third after comments by a representative from Stonewall. But there was trouble with the online edition, and specifically the *Times* paywall. Non-subscribers could see only a snippet: the featured image – me – and the opening sentences before the piece faded into an offer to take up a digital subscription. Yardley was characteristically blunt: 'It used to be fun being a tranny, but people have lost their sense of humour. All you get is this moaning and whining. We're caught in a right mess.'

While I agreed entirely with the sentiment, I would not have said it that way. But that mattered little in the minds of others who saw only the truncated piece. My picture was conflated with Yardley's words, and suddenly I was in trouble. The journalist and her editor both offered support, but in the transgender community there was consternation. Rapidly, I was becoming *persona non grata*. Not for opposing transgender rights – I had just called for those to be upheld in *The Times* – but for opposing the ideology. I was charged with heresy, but I was not convicted immediately. As the online jury deliberated, some suggested that I might have been misled or misreported by the journalist, and that there might be some other explanation.

Defending myself was not a palatable option. There was no way back, so forwards it was. I had already penned another column for the *Star* as part of a feature that debated self-ID.[28]

Two activists wrote in support, while two of us opposed it. I did not mince my words: 'a reckless proposal' was how I put it. But, while self-ID was not law, it had already worked its way into Labour Party policy. As far as the party was concerned, trans women were women and we could stand on all-women lists. We could even apply for the Jo Cox Women in Leadership Programme. Then Lily Madigan – a nineteen-year-old trans woman – was elected as a Labour Party branch women's officer. There was widespread outrage. I pitched my ideas to *The Times*; the editor asked for 450 words.

The opportunity was huge. This was not the time to hold back, and if I thought it, I said it. I reported the words of a Labour councillor who had supported Madigan's application. According to him, the party had decided that 'transgender women are women', and he 'fundamentally believed' that Lily was a woman. In *The Times*, I responded:

> People fundamentally believe lots of things but that does not necessarily make them true. We don't legislate on the basis of astrology or homeopathy, for example, yet the government is considering reforms to the Gender Recognition Act that may allow people to self-identify their legal sex based on their fundamental beliefs.[29]

I raised the flag for science and then dismissed the idea that Madigan would be an effective women's officer:

> To command respect, we need to ground our laws in scientific truth and in society. Science cannot be fooled.

The two sexes do have different roles in the propagation of our species and women's officers need to empathise with the issues that females face... Those of us socialised as boys need to think carefully before taking places in schemes designed to compensate the rather different formative experience of girls.

This time, the judgement of the online trans community was swift and uncompromising. There could be no more benefit of the doubt because there was no doubt. I had said what I thought under my own byline in *The Times*. Not only did I deny the central tenet of the faith – trans women are women – I had picked out individuals for criticism. My Facebook friends list shrank before my eyes, and online trans discussion groups vanished from view – I was excluded and blocked without explanation. I had been convicted of heresy and become an apostate to the true faith.

In real life, however, relationships were more durable. It is easy to demonise a disembodied avatar with words on a screen; it's harder when that person eats and drinks with you and comes alongside you when you need help. Members of the committee might have been disturbed by what I was writing in the press, but they also knew me as a human being. For the time being at least, my position on the TUC LGBT+ committee seemed secure.

4

AUTOGYNEPHILIA

I F transwomen are not women then what *are* we? It's one thing to dismiss the simplistic – and unprovable – notion that we have a gender identity, but quite something else to explain what is actually going on deep in our minds. Why do some men feel compelled to become women if we are not women already?

The question might be simple, but the environment is punishing. Too often the ferocious political debate is characterised by emotion and assertion, while reason and explanation are trampled underfoot. In such a difficult terrain for debate, assertions go unchallenged. Gender identity was an assumption, but so is the idea that there might be a single cause of transsexualism. Maybe we are trans for a host of different reasons? What is gender dysphoria – beyond a dissatisfaction with our gender – and what indeed is gender? When words are created, meanings are created with them. But if there is no foundation to those meanings then our thinking can rest on no more than fantasy. We need to do better than that if we are going to understand the human condition.

Sweeping aside the technical and poorly defined terminology that litters the political debate, five clear and objective truths remain.

- Human beings are mammals, a class of vertebrate animals in which the young feed on milk.
- Like other mammals, humans are sexually dimorphic – females produce eggs and males produce sperm – and an individual's sex is innate and immutable.
- Our sex affects both our physiology and our psychology. Male bodies are on average taller, stronger and more hairy than female bodies. At the same time, male minds are overwhelmingly attracted to female bodies, and vice versa. Yes, there are exceptions, but the differences between the sexes are clear and unmistakable.
- We are remarkably good at identifying the sex of other human beings, even if we cannot readily explain how we do it. What is the difference between a female face and a male face? We can distinguish them without the need for making measurements – if indeed we could even know where to put the ruler and protractor.
- Some human beings appear to have an insatiable urge to present as – and be perceived as – the other sex.

The clinical diagnosis has changed from 'gender identity disorder' to 'gender dysphoria', and it may change again to 'gender incongruence', but there is no need for specialist terminology. Why not use plain language that can be readily understood by anyone? Psychiatrists could simply note 'an insatiable need to present as the other sex', and then ask the question: why would anyone want to do such a thing?

But instead, the clinical language has created a new condition – sometimes called 'transsexualism' – that is treated with social transition, hormone therapy and gender reassignment surgery. Meanwhile, the underlying causes of gender distress, whether they are psychological or neurological, are overlooked, or perhaps even denied. In 2019, it was reported that 'transgender' was no longer recognised as a disorder by the World Health Organization.[1] A lack of curiosity about the sources of the distress has led to a focus on the treatment of its symptoms. That is hardly good medicine and not the usual practice. Doctors don't, for example, diagnose a disease called 'headache'; they view it as a symptom of any number of different conditions varying from the trivial – mild dehydration, perhaps? – to the very serious. Each of which needs different treatment.

Because there are different groups coming forward to seek help for this thing called 'gender dysphoria', it seems reasonable to suggest that the causes of their distress might not be the same. What indeed could possibly connect men who want to become women with women who want to leave womanhood behind? Even the male contingent can be divided into two distinct groups. Firstly, there is a cohort of feminine men who are sexually attracted to other males, and whose gender non-conforming behaviour extends back to childhood. The second group tends to come out suddenly in adulthood, often after marrying women, sometimes after fathering children, and usually to the surprise of those around them. I was in the latter category.

This is not new knowledge. Back in the 1980s, Ray Blanchard – an American–Canadian sexologist working at the Toronto Centre for Addiction and Mental Health – developed a somewhat controversial taxonomy of male-to-female transsexualism.[2] The first group he described simply as 'homosexual transsexuals' (HSTS), but it is the second group that interests me personally because it encompasses my own experience. A group needs a name – where would the transgender world be without labels? – and, in 1989, Blanchard coined the term 'autogynephilia'.[3]

In 2021, Blanchard told me that autogynephilia denotes 'a natal male's tendency to be sexually aroused by the thought or image of himself as a woman'. He added: 'In the Western hemisphere and English-speaking Commonwealth countries, the overwhelming majority of adult natal males presenting with gender dysphoria are of the autogynephilic type.'[4]

But what does this mean? How can this bizarre-sounding concept – 'love of myself as a woman', as it is sometimes described – cause that insatiable need to pass as a woman? Moreover, why did Blanchard's idea cause such a furore in the transgender community?

I believe that to answer these questions, we need to consider the legacy of human evolution, and in this case mind as well as body. In particular, what motivates men and women to present themselves differently in the first place?

Like other mammals, humans have evolved preferences and behaviours that have served us well, from finding sweet foods tasty, spiders scary and excrement disgusting, to finding potential mates enticing.[5] And just like other animals, male and female humans have experienced sexual competition and selection, which have resulted in the bodies and minds we know today.[6]

Differences in psychology go beyond sexual attraction.[7] Yes, overwhelmingly, men are attracted to women, and women are attracted to men. But sexual attraction requires potential partners to recognise one another and signal their fitness. Famously, peacock males have spectacular feathers that they use to attract peahens, but peafowl are far from unique. For humans, our attractive features that sexually signal to prospective mates include V-shaped torsos in men and women's permanent breasts.[8]

When resources allow, human sexual signalling can and does extend far beyond our bodies. Signalling is so ingrained in society that it hides in plain sight. As sexual beings, we show it in our clothing, hairstyles, make-up, even the way we walk, move and interact – and flirt – with each other. And while in many animals the male is the more colourful, women tend to be more adorned than men. Perhaps this is because, in contrast to most great apes, human fathers contribute to child-rearing; consequently, women need to attract high-quality, committed mates, and they compete for them.

It would be a mistake to dismiss all gender norms as arbitrary social conventions, with no intrinsic basis. We are animals, and our evolved instincts protect us, like they protect other species. Nurture will no doubt play its part, but when men and women display such distinct patterns of dress and presentation, we cannot ignore our nature. We are simply displaying our sexually attractive animal selves. But to recognise sexual signalling in humans is like being reminded that we are breathing. It might not be a commonly expressible concept, but we all participate and we are expected to conform. Those of us who are atypical in our signalling are noticed and labelled – 'queer', 'butch', 'effeminate', other less complimentary words. And now, arguably, 'trans'.

We are social beings, and in this game of life that we play with each other, we are constantly signalling our own sexual attractiveness and responding to the signals from other people. Millions of years of evolution have instilled in us the need to continue our species. Had it not, it is improbable that we would be here to ask why not. After our immediate needs for food and water, clothing and shelter have been addressed, the biological urge to procreate cannot easily be ignored.

At last we can make sense of what transgender people are doing, because we can articulate what most other adults are doing. Trans people wish to be perceived as attractive members of the opposite sex. We transition – changing our bodies and faces with surgery and hormones, our clothing and hairstyles, our make-up and adornments, our body hair and our voices, even our names. These are sexual signals. The way we present ourselves and wish to be seen is – as it is for other humans, indeed other animals – deeply and fundamentally connected to our sexuality. Far from a monolithic 'gender identity mismatch' set apart from sexuality, being trans is a basically sexual phenomenon that can have diverse causes – because human sexuality is also diverse.

Within the smorgasbord of human sexual interests lies autogynephilia – an arousal to the thought of oneself as a woman. Although how, precisely, autogynephilia arises has yet to be fully understood, we know that human beings are self-aware and self-conscious. If we believe we look good to others, then we feel good about ourselves. What if a wire in our brain got crossed, as it were, between our sense of what we seek out in a partner, and our sense of how we look to others? Conceivably this kind of cross-talk would result in an 'erotic-target-location error' directed towards our own body. We would desire to transform ourselves into our ideal partner.

The problem is self-evident. We are heterosexual males – and therefore evolved to tune in to signals given off by females – but the target of our sexual interest is a lamentably male body. This is a circle that cannot easily be squared. While other men might encourage their female partners to dress in a way they find particularly enticing, autogynephilic men have their own bodies as a canvas. Secret cross-dressing can then follow as surely as night follows day.

For some, transvestism – as it was once called – might satisfy, but the attraction for most men is not the clothing but the body it adorns. For autogynephiles, the compulsion to transition that body is then driven by one of the most powerful forces known to man – the male sex drive itself. Looking back on my own experience, I would go one step further and argue that my sex drive was short-circuited. In effect I was sex-signalling to myself. There was no resistance in the circuit, and nothing to stop me from becoming overwhelmed by my need to turn my body into the woman I longed to be.

But as with other males, our sexual interests are not restricted to a single body. In 1991, Blanchard pointed out that autogynephilia 'arises in association with normal heterosexuality but also competes with it'.[9] So we marry, and we form enduring relationships with women. All the time, however, that 'other woman' is hiding in the shadows – out of sight but not out of mind. Because, for autogynephiles, that other woman is us.

When other men might have extramarital affairs in their forties – perhaps in response to that biological urge to further distribute their genes – autogynephilic males transition. The parallels are unmistakable. The same selfish urges overpower the individual and become irresistible. Rightly we remain responsible for our actions, and the deleterious impact on those around us, but the biological impetus can be all-consuming – particularly if we have not the first clue what is actually going on.

It is superficially attractive to tell ourselves – and anyone who will listen – that we are women who have had the misfortune to have been born in the wrong body. That cannot possibly be our fault, can it? According to that well-rehearsed narrative, we then transition to put right what nature got wrong. The changes to our social presentation, our hormone regimes and ultimately our sex characteristics are not self-serving indulgences; instead they are the desperate measures we must take to become the women that we were supposed to be. We can frame ourselves as victims of circumstance, and look for sympathy and compassion in a society where other people genuinely want to be kind. It is a false narrative – nobody is born in the wrong body – but it is a fantasy that can hold if nobody thinks about it too hard.

The alternative is much harder to take. We are that other woman, and when we transition we are having an affair with her. It's no wonder, therefore, that autogynephilia is a topic few transsexuals are prepared to countenance. But it is part of the human condition and, if we hope to understand ourselves, we need to explore our nature with an open mind. Blanchard suggested four strands of autogynephilic sexual fantasy.[10] They may well occur together – just as other men's sexual interests can be varied and overlap – but listing them separately helps to understand what is going on in the mind of the autogynephile.

- Transvestic autogynephilia: arousal by wearing clothing more typically worn by women, or even the thought of wearing those clothes.
- Behavioural autogynephilia: arousal by doing something more typical of women or – again – thinking about carrying out those activities.
- Anatomic autogynephilia: arousal by the fantasy of having a normative woman's body.
- Physiological autogynephilia: arousal by the fantasy of having female body functions.

In some cases – and indeed when transition is not an option – the first two might suffice. The fantasy of having a female body can be maintained by disguising the male body with female attire, while stereotypically feminine activities – needlework? knitting? – can complete the illusion. Women looking on might well suggest that the autogynephile could at least do something useful and get on with the housework, but the focus is on self, not the wider world.

Clothes and activities can, however, only go so far. We are animals, and animals are attracted to bodies because it is bodies that reproduce. If medical and surgical transition is possible, then anatomic autogynephilia will drive a demand for it. It would be unlikely to stop there. No surgery – yet – can enable transwomen to menstruate, but if it became a thing, there would surely be a demand for it.

The driver is sexual arousal. If it were not for sex, it would make no sense for anyone to transition, and if it was not for sexual arousal it is unlikely that men would find the time, energy or resources to carry it through. Autogynephilic transition cannot be divorced from our sexuality, just as breathing cannot be separated from our need to respire.

Observations of autogynephilic transitions are a remarkable window into the male mind. While normal heterosexual men know what they like to see in a woman, those thoughts can be locked up in their own minds. Not so the autogynephile. When we transition, those thoughts are externalised in the changes we make to our bodies, and the way in which we dress them. We can see that in as much detail as we care to observe when viewing those transition picture books that many male transitioners have shared with the internet. The male erotic attraction to women's long hair, made-up faces and shapely bodies is undeniable when it's precisely those attributes that male transitioners adopt.

But what we observe in those picture books is hardly typical of women. The clothing, accessories, hair and make-up accentuate the impression of a female body often far beyond that projected by women. Shortly before I transitioned, Stephanie and I attended an event hosted by a trans group. It was late in the year; it was cold and it was dark. Stephanie was wearing trousers, as were almost all the women in the room. Not so some of the males who identified as trans. Actually, rather a lot of them. They were instantly recognisable by their skirts, which were at a length that might have been seen on women several years younger.

But that does not negate the theory; rather, it corroborates it. Heterosexual relationships involve two people: a male who would like his partner to wear revealing clothing, and a female who most likely would like to wear something far more comfortable and practical. In that electrical-circuit imagery – I am a physics teacher after all – the man is the cell and the woman is the load. The current flows, sometimes more and sometimes less, but there are two components in the circuit. Autogynephilic relationships involve just one – there is no partner and therefore no load – and the resulting short circuit can sometimes result in a spectacle: adult men prancing around the supermarket in miniskirts and high heels. It is an extreme parody of womanhood, flowing from the minds of the other sex.

Autogynephilia accounts nicely for transsexualism in heterosexual males, but we are only part of the story. The sexual focus for homosexual transsexuals – HSTS – is not the female body, but the male body and how to attract it. Characteristically, HSTS males are feminine in their nature and their interests, and their gender non-conforming behaviour is apparent from early childhood. While I was repressed by shame throughout my early years, an HSTS transitioner explained to me that 'it was just easier to be girly, and many people took me for a girl'. Transition then followed naturally: 'It was a label to describe something that I had already done.' There was no sense of shame, and none of the intricate and detailed planning that I had known. It is a different condition and a different experience.

Human sexuality is, however, more than a heterosexual–homosexual binary. What about bisexual males? Or asexual males? Indeed, there is a growing community of self-identified asexual people – they are the 'A' in the ever-lengthening alphabet soup, LGBTQIA+. Men can be sexually attracted to both sexes or neither, and nobody should be called to account for their sexual orientation. But among *non-homosexual* transgender-identified males, autogynephilia can also account for some of those different sexualities. The sexual focus for the autogynephilic male is himself – as a woman – and the need for others to perceive him as a woman. There is no reason why that cannot include the sex act itself. Blanchard suggested that autogynephiles who claim attraction to men are actually experiencing 'pseudo-bisexuality'.[11] They are not bisexual in the sense that other males might be bisexual. For them, their male partner validates their fantasy of being a woman. Essentially, the male sexual partner is a bit part in the autogynephile's focus on his own body.

In many cases, autogynephilia competes with normal heterosexual attraction. That is why autogynephiles often marry and then father children. For those who never transition, autogynephilia can remain hidden away: boxed-up inside the mind, perhaps like some unrequited love. But what if autogynephilia totally overpowers the external attraction? If sexual contentment can be found simply in the fantasy of having a female body, why bother involving any external sexual partners at all? Just as pseudo-bisexuality is distinct from typical bisexuality, this 'pseudo-asexuality' is distinct from typical asexuality, where the person feels no sexual attraction whatsoever.

Indeed, it is hard to understand why true asexuality needs to be included in the alphabet soup. Low sex drive may cause other problems – marital disharmony, perhaps? – and it may be linked to other psychological or physiological conditions, but it is hardly a problem in itself. Nor is there obvious scope for harassment or discrimination. Men and women can be single and without a sexual partner for any number of reasons, and it's not something that causes them to face abuse. On the surface, at least, there is no reason why asexuality should ever have become an equalities issue. But, nevertheless, self-identified asexual campaigners have made the supposed absence of a sex drive into a sexuality of its own. Not only does it have its own letter, it now has its own flag, and we hear about demands for 'asexual rights', as if the rights *not* to marry and *not* to have sex are denied to anyone, at least in the UK.[12] But while we might like to think that we can be self-sufficient and self-contained, we are social beings, and we need other people. Asexual campaigns begin to make sense, therefore, if they create communities with a sense of purpose and direction. We can all appreciate those things.

Bringing the focus of the discussion back to autogynephilia, the hypothesis is that an erotic-target-location error – our own bodies – causes the sexual attraction vector to point inwards. But the heterosexual mind does not want to see a male body. Clothing that body with typically female clothes might help to support an illusion, but illusions are less likely to satisfy when medical transition is available. In my own experience, once I knew that I *could* transition, I suddenly *needed* to transition. The compulsion overwhelmed me, but years passed before I accepted autogynephilia as the explanation.

Internally, I protested on three different fronts. First, it didn't feel like a sexual attraction – and certainly not all the time. Second, I was convinced that I needed to escape from being male. That was not congruent with the idea that I was being driven by male sexuality. The third was emotional, rather than rational, and the most significant. It was easy to see transition as a doorway to becoming my true self – there was no shame in that. But a response to my own sexuality? There was a mountain to climb before I could take on that concept.

But it was much easier to reject ideas that I did not like than to construct an explanation of my own. There was definitely *something* that compelled me to walk to that operating theatre at Charing Cross Hospital, and it seemed much bigger than mere sexuality. It had been around since I was three years old, and never left. When friends pushed me on it, I suggested that – as a child – I wanted to be seen as a girl. Then, in midlife, it had fulminated into an urgent need to present as a woman. Why? I was asked. I had no answers; I was no closer to understanding myself and – with no explanation for my compulsion – I was left in a state of deep dissatisfaction.

The stumbling block was my understanding of human sexuality. I had always viewed it as an add-on – something that first appeared at puberty and then made regular visitations, not always at my convenience. I was not in some perpetual state of arousal, so how could that continuous feeling of longing be explained by sexuality? But an essay written by another transsexual finally made me stop and think. 'Becoming What We Love' drew from existing literature and summarised the problem. The author, Anne A. Lawrence, pointed out that 'Blanchard's formulation [of autogynephilia] is rejected by some MtF transsexuals as inconsistent with their experience'. Absolutely! I thought – I was not doing this for sexual kicks. But, crucially, Lawrence added, 'This rejection, I argue, results largely from the misconception that autogynephilia is a purely erotic phenomenon. Autogynephilia can more accurately be conceptualized as a type of sexual orientation and as a variety of romantic love, involving both erotic and affectional or attachment-based elements.'[13]

This began to make sense. There were parallels with my experience of heterosexual attraction, for example to

Stephanie. The bonds that attach us are far stronger than the fickleness of my sex drive. After thirty years together I am constantly attracted to her for friendship and companionship, underpinned by a deep affection. We share our thoughts, our hopes and our lives. Sex was certainly part of the attachment, but our marriage relationship is so much more.

And so it is with autogynephilia. The analogy with an extramarital affair might help to explain why middle-aged men feel compelled to transition, but it does not convey the intimacy of the relationship. Because this affair was with myself, the person I had known – literally – for as long as I can remember and whom I knew better than anyone else. Over a decade later, I am not in a permanent state of arousal. When I get dressed for work, for example, I might wear clothes that are attractive – it's perfectly normal for human beings to want to look good – but I'm equally concerned that they are comfortable and suitable for teaching and learning to take place.

This broader view of interpersonal, and – in this case – intrapersonal relationships began to make sense, but it also brought fresh challenges. Not only did I fancy myself, according to Lawrence I was also in love with myself. What man, or indeed transwoman, admits to that? No wonder, perhaps, that Blanchard's ideas fuel bitter controversy among trans people and the wider LGBT community. Those who promote them have faced suspicion and cancellation. American psychologist J. Michael Bailey discussed autogynephilia in his 2003 book *The Man Who Would Be Queen* (sometimes referred to as *TMWWBQ*).[14] Complaints flooded in and Bailey was

86

investigated by his employer – Northwestern University. Prominent among his detractors was computer scientist Lynn Conway, who had transitioned in 1968. Ultimately, Northwestern found no basis for the complaints, but by then Bailey had resigned as chair of the psychology department.

Bailey's experience was covered by bioethicist Alice Dreger in her 2015 book *Galileo's Middle Finger*.[15] She described *TMWWBQ* as scientifically accurate, well intended and sympathetic. She had clearly not been the first to think that way. In 2004, *TMWWBQ* had been nominated as a finalist for a Lambda Literary Award. 'The Lammys' – as they are sometimes known – are awarded by the Lambda Literary Foundation to celebrate LGBT literature. But, perhaps inevitably, that nomination was subsequently withdrawn, the book condemned as transphobic, and Bailey pilloried for having had the audacity to write it. Dreger added that 'Bailey made the mistake of thinking that openly accepting and promoting the truth about people's identities would be understood as the same as accepting them and helping them'.

Conway certainly did not see Bailey's intervention as any sort of help and launched a crusade against him. Dreger documented the way in which Conway – who was then a member of faculty at the University of Michigan – developed what became an enormous website, hosted by the university, for the purpose of taking down Bailey and his ideas. This was personal and it was emotional – I could empathise: I have felt the same way myself.

In late 2016, when I first came across Bailey's work and Dreger's analysis, I sympathised with Conway. My transsexualism might not have been caused by a gender identity, but neither could I accept that it was a fruit of my sexuality. It seemed tacky, but worse it risked an association with transvestic fetishism. Transsexuals might have been the objects of pity, but transvestites were the targets of ridicule. Who wants to invoke that? The risk to my credibility was palpable, and in any case, it felt far more than a sexual kink. Of that I was certain. But Bailey's book not only promoted autogynephilia to a wider audience, it did so sympathetically. For that reason alone, *TMWWBQ* was a threat to my identity.

But why should I care about a book written by a university professor on the other side of the Atlantic? Dreger had the answer and she explained it beautifully.

To understand the vehemence of the backlash against Bailey's book, you have to understand one more thing. There's a critical difference between autogynephilia and most other sexual orientations: most other orientations aren't erotically disrupted simply by being labeled. When you call a typical gay man homosexual, you're not disturbing his sexual hopes and desires. By contrast, autogynephilia is perhaps best understood as a love that would really rather we didn't speak its name. The ultimate eroticism of autogynephilia lies in the idea of *really* becoming or being a woman, not in being a natal male who desires to be a woman.

So – essentially – my autogynephilia fuelled the need to deny my autogynephilia, and the stronger those feelings became, the greater was the need to deny them. The mere mention of the word could trigger another short circuit, and this one generated feedback of the type that causes shrieks and piercing whistles. But not in audio equipment: this cacophony ripped through my very psyche.

The truth stared me in the face. If I was not autogynephilic, why was I so troubled? The same could be said for Conway and all the other transsexuals who denounced Bailey's book, and then Dreger's analysis of it. But it didn't stop there. Autogynephilia ignites fury and fierce denial not only in transsexuals, but also in their proxies. Allies might not be torn apart personally by autogynephilia but few – I suspect – would want to defend this peculiar form of male sexuality.

But while the inward direction is certainly unusual, this is still male heterosexuality – something shared by half of humanity. We also share the same tensions. Pornography has been used as a release mechanism by rather more men than would perhaps care to admit it. But does the wrong sort of porn turn ordinary straight men autogynephilic? I would say no. Porn doesn't cause unusual sexualities; rather, it reveals them. Besides, in my personal experience, my fantasies of becoming the other sex predate my knowledge that pornography even existed.

It could also be argued that autogynephilic men – whose sexual focus is their own body – might on average consume more porn than other males, especially if they have no sexual partner. The internet has made pornography far more accessible than ever before, but the opportunity for internet sex goes far beyond recorded images. For a trans friend, virtual prostitution became an opportunity to be the woman of their fantasies in the company of men who were willing to pay for the privilege. But why should these parts of the internet *create* autogynephilia in the first place? Just as homosexuality appears to be hard-wired into some people, autogynephilia appears to be hard-wired into others.

Fundamentally, there is nothing to be gained by denying the truth of our sexuality apart from ignorance of what drives us. Self-acceptance, however, came slowly. During 2017 and 2018, initially with great reluctance, I set aside my objections, quelled the internal shrieking, and broke the cycle of denial. Then, for the first time in my life, I began to understand myself.

Transition, five years earlier, had certainly provided palliative relief from that insatiable urge to present as the other sex, because I was doing it every day. But it never gave me the freedom that I craved. Not only did I need to convince myself that I was a woman, I needed other people to believe it and – if that was not enough – to persuade myself that they really did believe it. Looking back, it was a fool's game that left me at the mercy of other people's words, thoughts and feelings.

Now, I really was free. I knew why I had transitioned, and I could explain it. Moreover, I no longer needed the rest of humanity to affirm the fantasy that I was somehow the opposite sex. If other people did not accept that I had changed my body because I was heterosexually attracted to it, that was their business, and it did not affect me. It sounds easy – it wasn't. It took me two years to admit it to myself, and then another year before I managed to articulate it to others, and finally write about it. Then, in February 2020, I asserted: 'Autogynephilia drove my own transsexualism. And I can attest that there is huge mental dissonance built up in the brain of a male who somehow is heterosexually attracted to their own body. This paradox can have a devastating effect on one's mental health.'[16]

But while I was free, others were distressed. Trans people viewed me with disdain. For them, this was still a love whose name they desperately did not want to hear spoken. However, I was increasingly detached from the trans community, so that was their problem rather than mine. Friends and colleagues meanwhile shrugged it off – why should they care about my inner musings? They had enough troubles of their own to worry about. But for Stephanie there was more trauma. Eight years ago, I had told her that I was really a woman; now I declared an unusual sexuality. Which was worse? From my perspective it was impossible to tell. This second journey of self-discovery was – just like transition – focused on self. Our relationship prevailed, but that was thanks to a remarkable woman – and that is her story rather than mine.

More years have now passed since the truth dawned, and a question has germinated in my mind. If I had known in 2012 what I know now, would I have transitioned? In short, the answer is no. I turned my life, and my family's lives, upside down because I thought I was some kind of woman. My mental health had deteriorated alarmingly, and I saw transition as the only possible escape from increasing psychological dysfunction. I knew about autogynephilia – it was discussed, denied and dismissed among trans people – but did not accept it. Had I done so, then the pressing need for transition might have abated. Life would probably have carried on much as it had done for the previous four decades.

The last ten years would have been simpler – certainly for Stephanie and our children – but, crucially, I would probably never have wrestled with the issues, and understood those inner drivers that had gripped me since early childhood. Self-awareness and self-acceptance would likely still have eluded me. Maybe I did need to learn the hard way?

5

PERCEPTION AND REALITY

Even throughout the time I imagined that I was some kind of woman, the evidence for my sex was indisputable. I was born with testes and male genitalia, and my subsequent sexual development was unremarkable. I can't recall ever having my chromosomes tested, but I would be astonished if they are anything other than 46,XY (typical male). The evidence is overwhelming: three children were born after I supplied the sperm. Two of those children were boys, and there was only one person from whom they could inherit their own Y chromosome – me.

But does that mean that I am a man? Biologically, yes – men are adult human males. But human societies do not routinely test anyone's chromosomes before they record their sex. On a more personal level, we use our instincts. Nobody needs a degree in genetics to tell the difference between men and women: we have had that skill since before the dawn of humanity. We share it with other species. My female cat knew the difference between tomcats and other queens, and she reacted to them differently. Indeed, a species where the individuals cannot perceive the opposite sex of their own kind is unlikely to contribute much further to evolutionary history.

Perception is crucial. If we hope to resolve the febrile transgender debate that has raged through Western societies for almost a decade, then we should first understand the role of perceived sex within human society. Otherwise, we risk an impasse. That war of words is encapsulated in that simplest of questions: 'What is a woman?'

Firmly dug into one set of trenches, the proponents of gender identity ideology argue that 'man' and 'woman' are identities to be claimed. A woman is anyone who utters those magic words: 'I identify as a woman!' It sounds progressive and liberating to allow anyone to find their own place in society, especially when new categories are created for those who feel they don't fit either of the existing ones. As well as 'non-binary', there is 'a-gender', 'neutrois', 'androgyne', 'gender fluid', 'genderqueer' – the list goes on. The BBC once explained to children that there were 'over 100 genders'.[1]

Facing them across no man's land – or should that be 'no person's land'? – are the defenders of biological reality. In 2018, British campaigner Kellie-Jay Keen-Minshull paid £700 to emblazon a dictionary definition on a billboard: 'woman – adult human female'.[2] The message was quickly removed amid outrage on social media. Keen-Minshull had seemingly achieved her objective – 'to start a conversation' – but was she correct? She was clear about what she thought:

she said that the idea that transwomen were women was 'preposterous'. But is it *useful* to describe us as men?

Utility matters – that is, useful language needs to be meaningful. A far simpler example might be our perception of the colour yellow. As a physicist I might claim that yellow light comprises a band of electromagnetic waves with wave-lengths between 565 and 590 nanometres. But I perceive it to be yellow because those waves trigger both the red-sensitive cones and the green-sensitive cones in the back of my eyes. A certain mixture of red light and green light that excites those cones in the same proportions would also look yellow. So we call it yellow and rarely even think about it. When computer monitors show a yellow image only a geek might describe the light by its RGB (red-green-blue) code of 255, 255, 0. As far as the rest of us are concerned, what matters is what we perceive. The image is yellow because it looks yellow.

Had medical science not enabled individuals to change their bodies to resemble the other sex, *perceived sex* might never have become an issue. But if, after hormone therapy and surgery, someone is widely perceived to be the opposite sex, is it *intelligible* to refer to them as their biological sex? This is not about 'being kind'; it is about using language that is readily understood. Away from the internet, where real bodies are involved, we need labels that help rather than hinder. Picture the scene: a stranger is trying to find me in a crowded room. Without knowing who I am, they ask for directions from a mutual friend who does know me.

'I'm looking for Debbie Hayton.'

'Ah, Debbie!' comes the reply. 'He is the tall man with the grey hair by the bookcase.'

'Where?'

My friend's response might have been scientifically accurate, but it's unlikely that the person seeking me out would link that information to a human being who looked more like a woman, certainly at first glance. Of course, they could have been provided with a full and complete description:

'Ah, Debbie… You see the person over by the bookcase with the grey hair who could be taken for a woman? That's Debbie. He is a male transsexual, by the way.'

But how realistic is that every time I might be pointed out in a crowd? Descriptive labels exist to make life easier, not to create greater complexity. We all have lives to live and work to do, and little time for endless discussions of transsexualism and gender reassignment. The simplest reply is of course what generally happens:

'She is the tall woman with the grey hair…'

Hard-wiring the words 'men' and 'women' to 'male' and 'female' is also unhelpful when describing some people with 'differences of sexual development' or DSDs, sometimes known as intersex conditions.

Complete androgen insensitivity syndrome – or CAIS for short – for example, affects people with XY chromosomes: they are born with testes that can produce testosterone.[3] Strictly speaking, their sex is male. But because their bodies do not respond to that testosterone, they are never virilised. Their genitals, therefore, appear female and they are registered as female at birth. During puberty, their bodies can and do respond to the oestrogen that circulates in both sexes and they can develop female secondary sex characteristics. Sometimes the first clue that they are not XX female is the absence of menstruation – they have no womb so they will never have a period – but of course menstruation is not a necessary condition to be a woman.

It is totally unhelpful – and probably extremely hurtful – to describe people with CAIS as men. This is a group that could not develop male secondary sex characteristics even if they wanted to. When XX females take exogenous testosterone, they develop male facial hair; their body hair thickens and their voices drop. For transmen, this is an important feature of their transition. But those changes only happen because their bodies are sensitive to testosterone. Individuals with CAIS are not: their bodies would ignore the injected testosterone in the same way that they ignored the testosterone produced by their own bodies. If someone with CAIS wanted to transition then they would have to live without the beard, deep voice and – perhaps – male pattern baldness that signals 'man' to the world. This is one group for whom the word 'man' would be a total misapplication.

If people with CAIS look like women, sound like women and are perceived by others to be women, then it makes sense to call them women: it is a useful label that has meaning. CAIS women are women, in other words.

We also have a dilemma when medical transition is possible, because the sense of *man* and *woman* can indeed change – or at least become ambiguous – in transgender people. In short, a meaningful transition can alter the way our sex is perceived. Are transwomen women after all, then? Clearly, we are the opposite sex to women. My reproductive system was, as far as I am aware, typically male, and it certainly worked as expected. But we could say that someone *perceived* to be an adult human female can be usefully referred to as a woman. Transitioning doesn't change our sex, but it doesn't *need* to change our sex to alter the way others perceive us, and naturally interact with us.

Perception matters – and, specifically, how we perceive each other. It is a pillar of human society and human civilisation. The first farmers in ancient Mesopotamia knew how to make babies, and they will have known which of their children would likely grow up into people who could best defend their land in combat, and which would gestate their grandchildren. Despite lacking any knowledge of chromosomes, they would have been able to divide their society into two kinds of people. In the millennia that have followed, little has changed. Human beings are remarkably good at distinguishing men from women, and boys from girls. We might not be able to explain in minute detail how we do it, but we all know the difference.

It's not just human beings – or cats. Individual members of sexually dimorphic species respond differently to male and female, and to do that they need to perceive the difference. Every winter, I watch the ducks on the pond pair off. They know which ducks to bond with. Their plumage has evolved to signal their sex, but it would be pointless if their brains had not evolved to notice it and respond to it. Human beings are also animals. We may be able to build cities and send men to the moon, but we share an evolutionary history with the other great apes, and ultimately the rest of life on earth. The way that we human beings recognise male and female – even the directors of the Apollo program who launched only one sex into space – is, presumably, not too dissimilar from the ducks.

This perhaps explains the stalemate in the debate between those who claim a woman is anyone who identifies as a woman, and those who claim the label applies strictly to adult human females. Neither side can prevail because both argue against our evolved instincts. We just *know* that a man with a full beard is a man – however he might choose to identify – and on the other hand a CAIS woman is *not* a man – despite her testes and XY chromosomes. Just as the word *yellow* is about colour perception, not wavelength, the words *man* and *woman* very often convey our instinctive perceptions of sex – which are neither social agreements, nor biological facts.

However, it does help us understand why the Gender Recognition Act did not cause significant controversy when it was enacted in 2004 and in the years that followed – the GRA brought the law in line with our perception. The first group to apply for GRCs were those who had already completed the process of gender reassignment. As the saying goes, if it looks like a duck, swims like a duck and quacks like a duck, then it probably is a duck – and we might as well call it a duck.

But was society right to have allowed those individuals to go through gender reassignment in the first place? Indeed, when hormone therapy and gender reassignment surgery became a reality in the 1950s and 1960s, governments had three options.

They could have prohibited gender reassignment treatments, or at least tried to. International agreements would have been needed. Early surgeries took place in Morocco, where Georges Burou developed his penile skin flap inversion technique at his Casablanca clinic. Transsexual writer Jan Morris was one of several British patients who came back home with a fait accompli between the 1950s and the 1970s. Only later was the operation available in Britain. Our government could decide to ban gender reassignment surgery in the UK but, while eager patients have the money to pay for it, the practice would continue elsewhere in the world. Today the destination of choice for GRS tourism is more likely to be Thailand. Could it ever be feasible – certainly in liberal societies – to force those people to conform to sexist stereotypes to ensure that they are always taken for their biological sex?

Or they could have just fudged it. Arguably that's what happened when those early transsexuals returned to the UK. Their birth certificates and passports were quietly changed to reflect the impression they made on those around them. They might not *really* be the sex they appeared to be but – back to the imagery of the ducks – it was easier to create a legal fiction that they were the opposite sex. But it did not take long for disputes to arise, even among a relatively small cohort of individuals.

Famously, in 1969 Arthur Corbett – the husband of April Ashley, another Casablanca patient – filed for an annulment of his marriage on the grounds that Ashley was actually a man. In the landmark ruling *Corbett* v. *Corbett* (1970), Lord Justice Ormrod held that 'because marriage is essentially a union between a man and a woman, the relationship depended on sex, and not on gender. The law should adopt the chromosomal, gonadal and genital tests. If all three are congruent, that should determine a person's sex for the purpose of marriage.'[4]

According to the judgment, it appeared to be the 'first occasion on which a court in England [had] been called on to decide the sex of an individual and, consequently, there is no authority which is directly in point.'[5]

Why was there no authority? Ormrod continued:

This absence of authority is, at first sight, surprising, but is explained, I think, by two fairly recent events, the development of the technique of the operation for vagino-plasty, and its application to the treatment of male transsexuals; and the decision of the Court of Appeal in *S v S (otherwise W) (No 2)*, in which it was held that a woman, suffering from a congenital defect of the vagina, was not incapable of consummating her marriage because the length of the vagina could be increased surgically so as to permit full penetration.[6]

Ormrod's judgment introduced a legal test for sex, and it drew a line between the creation of a neovagina in males and the correction of congenital defects in females. It also stopped the amendment – or falsification, depending on your point of view – of birth certificates issued in the UK. But plenty of fudge remained. The Passport Office continued to change the sex markers in British passports from male to female, and vice versa, on the basis of a letter from a medical practitioner confirming that the 'change of gender is likely to be permanent', whatever that meant.[7] Few people knew, and for a long time it seemed that fewer cared.

The third option – to codify properly the concept of legal sex and protect the rights of transsexuals in law – would have been a serious undertaking involving Acts of Parliament, informed by public debate and then, no doubt, finessed by test cases in the courts.

Let me be clear: any provision for members of one sex to be recognised in law or policy as members of the opposite sex has a major impact not only on those individuals but on the rest of society. In particular, the rights of women are vulnerable if men can identify into their sex class. Women's boundaries are meaningless if men can cut their own keys to open the gate.

In the years since 1970 there have been two key Acts of Parliament. The Gender Recognition Act 2004 – I would argue – was flawed from the outset, while the Equality Act 2010 is misunderstood. The recent attempt to introduce 'self-identification of legal gender' has been an unmitigated disaster all round, but, to understand why, we need to examine the GRA and Equality Act in turn.

From 2004, the GRA once again allowed transsexuals to change their birth certificates. That change in the law followed *Goodwin* v. *United Kingdom*, heard by the European

Court of Human Rights in 2002.[8] Christine Goodwin was a 'post-operative male to female transsexual' who wanted to marry a man. Ultimately the court found that the UK was in violation of Articles 8 and 12 of the European Convention on Human Rights – respectively, the right to respect for private and family life, and the right to marry.[9] But – crucially – the judgment assumed that Goodwin had 'assimilated'. Essentially, the court held that if someone is perceived to be a woman, it is perverse for the law to treat them as a man.

Perhaps so, but the language used by the GRA was somewhat different: 'A person of either gender who is aged at least 18 may make an application for a gender recognition certificate on the basis of living in the other gender.'[10] But what can it mean to 'live in the other gender'? Is there a certain way in which people of a particular gender are supposed to live?

Had those drafting the bill talked about 'being routinely perceived to be the other sex', then some of the subsequent problems might have been averted. That wording would likely have been unpopular with both sides of the debate. Firstly, it would have introduced a 'passing test'. While we can all distinguish between men and women, we use instinct rather than a set of rules. Transgender activists would also no doubt protest that a woman is anyone who identifies as a woman. On the other hand, feminist campaigners would hold that only biological females can be women. But – and this is crucial – the law would have merely codified those instincts on which we rely every time we meet someone new.

Six years later, the Equality Act included the protected characteristic of 'gender reassignment'. Just like the GRA before it, there was no requirement for transsexuals to have actually undergone any surgery or, for that matter, any medical treatment at all. The wording was vague: 'A person has the protected characteristic of gender reassignment if the person is proposing to undergo, is undergoing or has undergone a process (or part of a process) for the purpose of reassigning the person's sex by changing physiological or other attributes of sex.'[11]

'Other attributes'? That definition could include anyone who wandered even slightly from social gender norms. But that is the point: the tragedy is that the law is so often misinterpreted. As Kemi Badenoch, the UK minister for women and equalities, clarified in 2022: 'the Equality Act is a shield, not a sword. It is there to protect people of all characteristics.'[12] Indeed, an individual does not need to actually claim the characteristic. Perception is enough. According to UK government guidance, the Equality Act provides 'protection for people discriminated against because they are perceived to have, or are associated with someone who has, a protected characteristic'.[13]

What mattered to those lawmakers was how we are perceived and, if we are treated less favourably as a result, then we are protected by the law. This makes sense. If, for example, I am perceived to be homosexual, and I suffer harassment as a result, then I am protected by the characteristic of sexual orientation. As Badenoch confirmed, the law protects me as an individual; it does not provide me with extra rights according to how many protected characteristics I can chalk up. Sadly, that point is lost on many and the law is misunderstood.

But worse was to follow. Since Yogyakarta in 2006, and certainly since around 2015, a new type of thinking has emerged. In this world, 'gender reassignment' – something we *do* – has been replaced by 'gender identity' – something we *are*. Essentially, in this age of identity politics, the verb *to do* has been replaced by the verb *to be*. People can choose to identify however they like and, the thinking goes, those identities should be enshrined in law.

'Gender identity' has found its way into the statute books in multiple jurisdictions. For example, in 2011, the US state of Massachusetts determined that

> 'Gender identity' shall mean a person's gender-related identity, appearance or behavior, whether or not that gender-related identity, appearance or behavior is different from that traditionally associated with the person's physiology or assigned sex at birth. Gender-related identity may be shown by providing evidence including, but not limited to, medical history, care or treatment of the gender-related identity, consistent and uniform assertion of the gender-related identity or any other evidence that the gender-related identity is sincerely held as part of a person's core identity.[14]

This unprovable and unfalsifiable statement clearly opened the door to bad actors. Presumably the lawmakers in Boston knew that, because they added: 'provided, however, that gender-related identity shall not be asserted for any improper purpose.'

But who is to say which purposes are proper and which are improper? Taking people at their word means taking them at their word, whatever their motives. Watching the political debate play out at Westminster and elsewhere, I often sense a process of triplethink among MPs and policy-makers who set themselves up as eager trans allies. They seem to hold simultaneously three mutually incompatible ideas on the matter:

1. We should be allowed to self-identify our gender.
2. At least where trans people are concerned, law and policy should follow gender identity rather than biological sex.
3. Adverse consequences would be insignificant.

The first two in isolation might form a coherent view-point – but not all three together because the potential for abuse stares us in the face. If abusive men will train for the priesthood to access their victims, why would they not tick a box on a form to register a change of gender in order to circumvent women's boundaries?

One and three are consistent – at least for wider society – but only if policymakers prioritise biology, and gender remains a purely personal matter.

Even two and three hold, at least to some degree. If, that is, there are sufficient checks and balances to weed out bad actors, those with certain comorbid disorders and those who have made no attempt to resemble the opposite sex. Arguably that was the position taken by the GRA. Even psychiatric reports rely on whatever details the patient chooses to disclose to the clinician, but trans people can still be identified objectively by how they present themselves. Gender *reassignment* – to use the language of the Equality Act – is something tangible, unlike any assertion of gender *identity*. As gatekeeping went it was perhaps minimal, but it was better than nothing.

But the three together produce an insoluble conundrum. If law and policy follow self-identified gender then there will be adverse consequences. Outrageous examples of male rapists being sent to women's prisons in England and Scotland were both predictable and inevitable.[15] As was the increased suspicion of transsexuals. Among those 'policy priorities for transgender equality' – to appropriate the title of the meeting that delivered the first of the four bombshells of 2016 – self-identification of legal gender should never have left the starting blocks. It is poor policy that has caused untold harm.

Clouding the issue has been that verb shift from *to do* to *to be* – from gender reassignment to gender identity. Few people seemed to notice and, to my mind, even fewer understood the consequences.

The impact on wider society is exemplified in the sudden proliferation of preferred pronouns. Increasingly, it seems, email signatures, internet profiles, even identity badges, are no longer complete without a nod to pronouns. In some places, the practice has become so ubiquitous that it is difficult to be a conscientious objector – especially when it seems so harmless. But beneath the appearance of a kind gesture, power is transferred, and in the direction of the badge-wearer.

No longer does the observer have the freedom to perceive which sex-based pronouns best describe the human being standing in front of them: they are now expected to read the label and follow the instructions. When I transitioned – just over a decade ago – pronoun badges were unknown, and for many transsexuals they would also have been unwanted. Pronouns were the acid test of a successful transition. When strangers described me using the pronouns *she* and *her* – without being prompted – I knew I was *doing* it well enough. Declaring my pronouns would have defeated the exercise.

Even worse is the potential impact on trans people who are still in the closet. Declarations of pronouns place them in an excruciating dilemma. Picture the scene – one of those business meetings that now start with pronouns:

'My name is Alan and my pronouns are *he/him.*'

The precedent is set.

'Hi, I'm Barbara and my pronouns are *she/her.*'

'Hello, my name is Colin and I use *he/they* pronouns.'

'My name is Debbie, and I am not declaring any pronouns.'

I always refuse. If this had happened during the first forty-three years of my life, what pronouns could I have shared? *She/her?* And come out as trans in a business meeting, perhaps before I had even told my wife? Or declare the very pronouns that were exacerbating my dysphoria? So, just in case there is anyone else sitting around the table struggling in silence with gender dysphoria, I neither share pronouns nor fudge it by omission.

Offering pronouns may seem to be kind, but it can so quickly become an expectation and an imposition. Others can use whatever pronouns they like for me. I have no need to compel anyone else's speech. I am still surprised when I am not 'read' at fifty paces: I'm almost six feet tall, my shoulders are broad and my voice broke in adolescence – but people take me as they find me. Transsexualism is not on most people's minds when they meet someone new. The choice is instinctive: man or woman? And the balance tips one way or the other. 'Reasonably well-passing transsexuals', to quote a friend of mine, do not need to wear pronoun badges.

A new colleague who was still unaware of my past once challenged me – ever so nicely – for not wearing my pronouns. She suggested that it might be a kind gesture. I asked her to explain.

'Well, Debbie, it's really helpful to trans people. If we share our pronouns, they do not stand out when they share theirs.'

'Is that so?'

The irony was delicious, and the temptation to say more was almost unbearable. But I was there to do a job, not to discuss pronouns or transsexualism. If the goal was to pass, then I had done so with distinction. But times have changed, and rapidly. To the adherents of gender identity, the verb *to do* plays second fiddle: *to be* is in the ascendancy, and social presentation is secondary. For them, pronoun badges have become de rigueur.

To my colleague ('*she/her*'), the badge was redundant – I read her as female anyway. But where does this leave the self-identified trans person who is clocked at a hundred paces? Perhaps they make no attempt to pass as the opposite sex? Perhaps they think a gender identity badge can be a substitute for the process of gender reassignment? That is the message that is being delivered, especially to young people.

Online, where they can exist as a handle and an avatar – and communicate by text and emojis – it might seem to work. But it's hardly a realistic foundation on which to build real-world relationships where bodies are involved. Whatever the badge might say, we evolved to assess the sex of those bodies. If the messages clash, the observer must choose – follow the badge or trust their instincts? When the badge wins, the wearer achieves something remarkable. They control the speech of other people.

If the assessment of sex were purely rational, and mediated solely by language, then Orwellian changes to the meaning of words might even control the thoughts of others. But it is an instinct that we share with other species. It predates language, perhaps even rational thought: we do not merely think about the sex of other people, we feel it. As long as human beings have human bodies, those who think that their assertion of gender identity will displace other people's assessment of their biological sex are ultimately doomed to disappointment.

But that has not stopped people trying to impose these ideas. Campaigning groups including the International Lesbian, Gay, Bisexual, Trans and Intersex Association (ILGA), the Human Rights Campaign in the United States and Stonewall in the UK have been at the vanguard.[16] Together with international NGOs such as Amnesty International, they have lobbied extensively.[17] Parliamentarians have capitulated, enshrining gender identity into law. Where there has been resistance – for example in the UK – policymakers have been encouraged by some campaigners to 'get ahead of the law'.[18]

Their tactics were exposed in 2019, when the 'Dentons document' came to light.[19] This report, 'Only adults? Good practices in legal gender recognition for youth', was authored by Dentons (who claimed to be the world's largest law firm by number of lawyers) along with the Thomson Reuters Foundation and the International Lesbian, Gay, Bisexual, Transgender, Queer and Intersex Youth and Student Organisation (IGLYO). It had as its focus youth, and helping campaigners to change the law to allow children to change their gender (and hence their legal sex) without the approval of adults or authorities, and especially – it seemed – their parents. According to the authors: 'It is recognised that the requirement for parental consent or the consent of a legal guardian can be restrictive and problematic for minors.' Should parents disagree, the authors added, 'states should take action against parents who are obstructing the free development of a young trans person's identity in refusing to give parental authorisation when required.'

It was – and remains – a troubling document. But it shone a light on the tactics of the lobbyists: 'Get ahead of the government agenda... intervene early in the legislative process and ideally before it has even started.' Gender recognition – for all ages and without safeguards – was hardly likely to be a popular cause. Campaigners were therefore advised to tie their campaigns to more popular reform – as happened in Ireland, where self-identification was introduced along with equal marriage – and to limit press coverage.

Whatever the motives of the authors of the report, or indeed the campaigners they were attempting to support, these comments should have raised red flags. Why the need to shut out parents, and keep things quiet? Even more worryingly, which groups of adults might be keen to take advantage of such a campaign?

Too many governments and policymakers simply capitulated. Within workplaces it has maybe even achieved the remarkable feat of uniting HR and trade unions in a single way of thinking: in their minds, how we feel about ourselves displaces other people's perceptions of us. If that were actually the case, the very foundations of human society would be at risk.

We have always cared how others have seen us and thought about us. In the very distant past it was vital: individuals needed the goodwill of the tribe to survive. With larger societies came organised religions with their codes of ethics, and expectations of conduct. Those who complied were seen as good people, and those who cared about being considered good were more likely to prosper. Our basic needs are perhaps less obvious in modern societies – governed by policy, served by institutions and policed without fear or favour – but we have not evolved into a new species.

Human beings still need to belong to a group, but the groups have changed rapidly. They have also become virtual – mediated by the internet – in a way that would have been unimaginable only a few years ago. One group is the LGBT+ community. The plus is crucial. As the initials have crept across the page – LGBTQQIP2SAA, according to one British newspaper[20] – this world is no longer the preserve of people who happen to be attracted to their own sex. It is inclusive of everyone, and it is evangelistic in nature. The two Qs are an open door. 'Queer' – still considered a slur by some homosexuals – is now claimed by some heterosexuals, who perhaps want to celebrate unusual sexualities of a different kind. Meanwhile, literally anybody could be 'questioning'.

Public services have been captured. Hospitals fly Pride flags – 'to demonstrate inclusive care for all' – while the police paint rainbows on the sides of squad cars.[21] One deputy chief constable said: 'It is there to try and give confidence to our LGBT+ community, but also to other under-represented groups.'[22] Really? Why, for example, should religious minorities be encouraged by LGBT+ symbols?

Some constabularies have gone even further. Alongside the Crown – the very symbol of the state – Stonewall logos have appeared on police cars.[23] If any organisation has been doing the capturing, it is Stonewall UK. This campaigning organisation claims its Workplace Equality Index to be 'the UK's leading benchmarking tool for LGBTQ+ inclusion in the workplace'.[24] Every year it publishes a 'top 100 Employers for LGBTQ+ people'. In 2022 the list included the police forces of Avon and Somerset, Leicestershire, Surrey and Sussex.[25]

The aim – presumably – is to be seen as good people and good organisations. If the LGBT+ community has morphed into a quasi-religious movement, then organisations like Stonewall have provided the structure and written the creeds and the dogma – for example: 'Trans women are women, trans men are men and non-binary identities are valid.' It's a statement I repudiate, but one that has become so ubiquitous I have learned it by heart. That central belief – that we all have a gender identity that determines whether we are men, women or something else – is fundamental. It displaces science and – if sex becomes unmentionable as a human category – demolishes women's boundaries and their sex-based rights. Ironically it also defines all human sexuality as attraction to gender identity rather than to the sex of a person, denying the basis of gay and lesbian existence.

The parallels with traditional religion are unmistakable. There is a priestly class – trans people – who are deemed to have some special knowledge about their gender identity. Politicians and policymakers defer to the demands of the trans lobby like their predecessors accommodated the requirements of the Church. Children are educated in this belief structure, and adults expected at least to go along with it if they want to be seen as worthy people.

In not much more than a decade, this new faith – gender identity ideology – has gripped our society. Those who deny it are viewed like dissidents in authoritarian religious states. Being labelled as a bad person has consequences. J. K. Rowling is perhaps the most high-profile objector: she has received death threats for her reasonable views. Dissenting politicians have been subjected to censure from within their parties, while ordinary people have received appalling abuse for simply stating the truth – human beings cannot change sex.

Continuing the analogy, those of us who leave the faith are apostates, and gender identity ideology treats its defectors like some religious cults treat theirs. We are deserters, heretics, even traitors; we are seen to be bad people who need to be removed from positions of influence, and silenced. If my piece in *The Times* about Lily Madigan had been a one-off, it might have been overlooked as an aberration. But as I continued to speak out, and find platforms in the press, my position on the TUC LGBT+ committee became increasingly uncomfortable, and two years later – in the autumn of 2019 – I found myself the subject of a disciplinary investigation by the TUC.

6

GENDER IDENTITY
TO GENDER APOSTASY

THE LGBT+ sector was my entry route into union work at a national level, but it did not constrain me for long. In the spring of 2018, I pushed on another door. I was elected to the NASUWT National Executive, and I became a national executive member, or NEM. A vacancy had arisen and I had put my name forward. The colleagues whose support I secured knew that I was transsexual, but nobody made an issue of it. I had proved my ability to represent the union at a national level in one context, and representation, together with negotiation, is a transferable skill.

I was thrust into a strategic role without much training and even less pay – NEMs are volunteers. Some are released by their employers, who continue to pay them a full-time salary while they attend meetings during the school day; I was not. However, I did have a part-time teaching contract so I had the time if not the money. The NASUWT organises in thirty-four districts across the UK, rather like constituencies.[1] Within my own West Midlands district, I supported local activists and led members who were in dispute with their employer. The job was intense. I've stood on a picket line outside one school at 8 a.m. before dashing to my own school to teach my pupils, then driving to a third school to negotiate with another employer to try to secure 'sufficient progress in talks' to avoid further strike action in my district.

On top of all that, there was the National Executive Committee itself. MPs go to Westminster; NEMs gather at the union HQ just south of Birmingham. Once a month we met for a full day of committee meetings and plenary debates. While we talked with great concern about the work–life balance of our members, we put in long sessions, sometimes extending well into the evening. Breaks would often be overrun by urgent casework. Hectic did not begin to describe the experience. I once dashed from a committee meeting to dispute talks in a nearby school before rushing back to a plenary debate, while taking emails and calls from activists in my district.

The work was certainly intense, but it was also enjoyable. It stretched me in ways that the LGBT+ sector did not. Joining the executive as a transsexual was not a success criterion; what mattered was whether I could negotiate better conditions for my members and help to develop effective union policy. The most important right that trans people have secured is – in my view – to be treated no less favourably than anyone else. During my time on the executive, that was a right I enjoyed totally. I was there as a teacher and I represented the members in my district in the same way that my colleagues represented theirs. However, it was because I was trans that I was already sitting on a TUC committee and meeting senior officials of my own union, other unions and the TUC itself. Without those experiences, I might never have considered running for the executive. It was my transsexualism that opened doors, and put me in a position of privilege.

I continued to represent the NASUWT on the TUC LGBT+ committee. One key role of that committee was to oversee the organisation of the annual TUC LGBT+ conference. That was a two-day affair at TUC Congress House, timed to coincide with Pride in London. Motions were debated often without dissent – there was generally very little controversy in debate. We would speak with one voice in support of worthy causes and then rise in the same sense of unity to deplore atrocious practices. Each year, conference would call on the committee to do many things – not that we had much power. While we could, for example, ask TUC officials to support a solidarity campaign for LGBT+ workers in countries where it was illegal to be gay, our influence on the governments who were oppressing those workers was close to zero.

Conference also elected the committee for the following year, albeit from a list of nominations already received from unions. Nominees tended to be elected unopposed, often with vacancies left unfilled. The key contest was not for people but for policy. Every year, delegates selected one motion from the LGBT+ conference agenda that would be sent to the next TUC Congress, where it would be debated a second time. There, actual policy was made. Unless Congress kicked out the motion – but who would dare say no to the LGBT+ lobby? – a key strand of TUC policy was in the hands of the delegates at the LGBT+ conference. In July 2018, it was clear that self-identification was in the ascendancy, and only one motion was ever in the running.

Ultimately listed as Motion 41 in the final 2018 TUC Congress agenda, 'Support for gender self-declaration' called on the TUC General Council to 'campaign for a simplified, free, statutory gender-recognition process based on self-declaration'.[2] But it was three words (in parentheses) from the next paragraph that would – four years later – come back to bite me personally: 'We support the right of all women (including trans women) to safe spaces and the continuation of monitoring that can help identify discrimination against women and men.'

I sat through both debates, but only voted once. As a trans member of the LGBT+ committee, I chaired the session at the LGBT+ conference during which the motion was called for the first time. The voting – by show of hands – appeared to be unanimous, so my casting vote was moot. I disagreed with the motion, but I nevertheless chaired the conference professionally and impartially, not that there were any contrary views expressed from the podium. Instead, we all listened to a series of angry speeches. The target of much of the vitriol, however, was not the government or those who genuinely opposed the rights of LGBT people. Instead, conference's outrage was directed squarely at a group of trade unionists who had recently penned a letter to the *Morning*

Star – ironically, to call for an improved climate of debate around the Gender Recognition Act.

The letter cited a series of recent incidents where women who opposed self-identification had been subjected to abuse and intimidation.[3] The writers then pointed out that

> these cases are part of systematic attempts to shut down meetings organised by women at which they can discuss potential legislative changes and the impact these may have on any sex-based rights already enshrined in law.
>
> They draw the whole of our progressive movement into disrepute.
>
> Some trans rights activists even continue to justify the use of violence, meaning that many women are simply too frightened to attend meetings that are both public and lawful in order that they may discuss their own rights.

The letter was signed by 153 women and men, including two general secretaries – Len McCluskey of Unite and Mark Serwotka of the Public and Commercial Services Union (PCS). The signatories explained that they did not support a particular position; rather, they 'publicly and unequivocally condemn[ed] the use of violence or tactics of intimidation on this issue'.

In the conference hall, the contempt for all 153 signatories was palpable. And it had not gone unnoticed that my signature was halfway down the list. We were painted as bigots, and standing not in opposition to violence but against the rights of trans people 'to exist'. Some of the speeches

included barbed remarks about the enemy within our movement, 'even people in this room'. Ho hum! I thought, before
announcing: 'That's three minutes, delegate, please can you
now draw your speech to a close.' At lunchtime, I was told
rather brusquely that some trans delegates had been unable
to attend the morning's debate because they felt unsafe in the
room while I sat in the chair. The TUC officials were perhaps
rather relieved that the chair was due to rotate to one of my
colleagues before the start of the afternoon session, but some
delegates demanded redress. Eventually the militants were
assuaged by being allowed to bring a point of order when
conference reconvened after lunch.

I was asked if I wanted to be absent from proceedings.
'Absolutely not,' I replied. This was something I wanted to
see for myself. As delegates drifted back into the debating
chamber, I took my place among the NASUWT delegation.
The atmosphere was electric, and what happened next was
almost theatrical. From the chair, my committee colleague
called for order. Immediately, a voice from the back of the
room boomed out, 'Point of order!' One thing transwomen
rarely lose is a voice that fills an auditorium and makes people
listen. This particular comrade was also wearing clicky heels;
the walk to the front was audible in a different way. I wasn't
named – but my transgressions were read out. A letter writer,
conference was told, was in this very room. The faux shock
was palpable. A couple of hundred pairs of eyes looked my
way. The complainant continued: the letter writers were an
anathema; we were everything that this inclusive conference
was not. Inclusion had limits, it seemed.

Despite everything, I could empathise with the complainant. Five years earlier I might have led such a protest myself. By 2018 I had become sufficiently confident in who I was not to be troubled by those with differing opinions. But back in early transition – 2013, say – when I could not begin to explain to myself why I had transitioned, any challenge to my fumbling assertion 'Because I am a woman' felt like a personal attack. As I sat in Congress House, I found myself listening to someone who was hurt as much as they were angry.

That didn't change the atmosphere in the room, though. I felt about as welcome as a visiting football supporter who had been identified and publicly called out in the enclosure reserved for home fans. The support from my own delegation was solid – they closed ranks around me because I was one of their own – but as the point of order came to an end, some other delegations joined in a standing ovation. They were not cheering me! As I turned to the next motion in the agenda, I had to stifle a chuckle at the absurdity of the situation. Our letter had condemned the use of violence or tactics of intimidation. There might not yet have been any violence at Congress House – that would happen in a committee meeting the following year – but intimidation percolated through the room. However, filled with their own self-righteousness, those responsible were glibly unaware.

Probably wisely, I made no further contributions from the podium, but I endured the whole afternoon session. Despite further protests from the floor, the TUC announced that the nominations for the following year's committee were closed – and had been for months – so I was elected unopposed to the TUC LGBT+ committee for a further year. Meanwhile 'Support for gender self-declaration' was sent to be debated at the TUC Congress, which, in September 2018, returned to Manchester – the city where the movement had begun 150 years earlier.

That year – 1868 – the first meeting of the TUC resolved to hold an annual congress, 'for the purpose of bringing the trades into closer alliance, and to take action in all Parliamentary matters pertaining to the general interests of the working classes'.[4] This was the movement that would champion the underpaid women chain-makers of Cradley Heath, who withdrew their labour in 1910, and the *Made in Dagenham* women, who went on strike for equal pay at the Ford car plant in 1968.[5] But, in 2018, Congress would be presented with a motion that would throw open the category of 'woman' to anyone who claimed to feel like one.

I took my place within a rather more senior NASUWT delegation led by the national president. Our first task was to meet as a delegation to determine our collective attitude to each motion. I had prepared my arguments against Motion 41 carefully, and I made a passionate case explaining why gender self-declaration was unhelpful to everyone – trans people included. I lost. Unions are by their nature collective bodies, and we decided to support the motion. Subsequently I found myself in Congress itself listening to the second debate on gender self-declaration. The same arguments were reprised. Trans people were oppressed and marginalised, we heard, and only by sweeping away the horrors of intrusive and demeaning medical gatekeeping could they be made whole.

That was the gist of it. Anecdotes were recalled, and Congress sympathised. Amid the groupthink, one of my NASUWT colleagues made a courageous speech defending the rights of individuals to stand up and say what they believed in. No names were mentioned but the glances in the room were directed my way.

Earlier, I had spoken with protestors outside the building. A group was handing out materials produced by the organisation Fair Play for Women. 'Hands off my rights,' they declared. Absolutely! They were right to be concerned and right to stand there, talking to delegates as they arrived for the session. Those chain-makers and Ford workers of earlier generations had been exploited not because they felt like women but because they *were* women. It was not an oppression that anyone could identify out of – not then and not now.

As the debate drew to a close, it was abundantly clear that Congress would not stand in the way of 'Support for gender self-declaration'. On one of the most fundamental pillars of human society – the distinction between men and women – the trade union movement had been captured by gender identity ideology. First the TUC LGBT+ conference and now the TUC Congress itself voted overwhelmingly to approve the idea that 'all women' included transwomen. Had the vote been on a knife-edge I might have thought twice, but I was in Manchester to represent not what I thought but what my union thought; my hand went up with the rest to approve the motion by an enormous majority.

My vote was observed and noted by those who had been watching me, but it did not relieve the pressure I faced within the union movement. I might have voted for self-declaration, but everyone knew I didn't actually believe in it. Of far greater concern to me, however, was the pressure on my workplace. There, my livelihood was at risk. If I had known at the outset how prominent I would become in the gender debate, I might have taken more precautions. I certainly would not have advertised my workplace on my social media profiles. My opponents found it all too easy to identify the school where I worked, and to whom complaints should be addressed.

Initially the outrage came from just one side of the dispute. Not all the women campaigning against self-identification appreciated my involvement, and some saw me as part of the problem. But they didn't try to cause trouble for me at work. Not so the LGBTQIA+ brigade and their allies. My school would tweet out the under-fifteen sports results and targeted replies would come in. 'Why are you employing a transphobic teacher?' summed up the attitude from the complainants; it was very nasty.

My colleague who monitored the notifications on the school's official Twitter account heard accusations that I was an online bully, a danger to children and an apologist for paedophilia. When transgender activists took a dislike to something I had tweeted they would tag in the school as they announced their displeasure. Their passive-aggressive outbursts were almost comical at times, but the intent was deadly serious. These people wanted to see me out of work and – as they became increasingly bold – I feared that they would stop at nothing.

The pressure was on me, but it was also on my employer. Tagging in my school, one activist tweeted: 'DH is a danger to all children,' adding: 'at this point you have to presume in still employing DH that the school don't [*sic*] care about children either.' Social media attacks were all too common. On another occasion, someone tagged the school before announcing: 'Why do you continue to condone the actions of this vile anti-trans, attention seeking individual. If you think that trans people can't be transphobic then you are part of the problem.'

Then there were the emails. These I heard about second-hand. If they didn't go straight to my headteacher, the reception desk forwarded them on to him. This delightful epistle appeared at 9.52 a.m. on 20 March 2019:

Hello,

I'm writing to express my deep concern about Debbie Hayton's continual harassment and bigotry towards transgender females on twitter. She provokes anti-trans feelings and mis-represents the trans community .

She has sided with several pseudo-feminist and anti-trans groups on twitter , and has had several of her inflammatory posts removed .

I wish to remain anonymous, but thought you should be aware of her activities and how they might reflect on your school .

I appreciate your time in reading this .

Thank you

The unusual punctuation – those spaces before the commas and full stops – suggested that the writer was a former teacher, who later tweeted: 'I did write to Hayton's school last year to complain about her bigotry and comments on Twitter, and how it may spill over into her classroom . They said they would look into it[.]' Actually, that email had gone straight to the police, along with the rest. The persistent harassment could have ended my career, but the school, which had supported me through transition, also protected my right to engage in legitimate political campaigning. The support from my employer was genuine, meaningful and ongoing. But the online tempest was another world to my day job. I was employed to teach physics, and that was my focus in school. Mostly, my pupils were oblivious. Only once was I ever asked about it in class. A pupil wanted to know why my Twitter account was verified. 'Because as well as teaching you, I write articles for the press. But enough of that,' I added. 'We need to get to grips with electromagnetic induction.' He shrugged and returned to his worksheet.

By then I was writing regularly for *The Spectator* and UnHerd, with occasional pieces in *The Times*, the *Daily Telegraph*, the *Morning Star* and elsewhere. Remarkably, my byline once appeared in *The Times* and the *Morning Star* on the same day.[6] Proof indeed that this was an issue that cut straight across traditional party lines.

Occasionally, parents contacted the school to commend my writing and the stance that I was taking. During one Year 12 parents' evening, a father came to my desk. I had taught his daughter in previous years, but she had decided not to continue with physics in the sixth form. He came straight to the point. 'Dr Hayton, I just wanted to say how much I appreciate the pieces you write in the press.'

I asked him to mention it to the headteacher as well. My detractors didn't think twice before also targeting him. Online chatter suggested that we had both been reported to the Teaching Regulation Agency (TRA), the body responsible for regulating the teaching profession.[7] The TRA holds misconduct hearings and has the power to bar people from teaching. Potentially, both our livelihoods were at stake.

It's all too easy for anonymous complainants to make trouble by raising allegations. They may be totally unfounded and they may be malicious, but they still need to be investigated. One came into the Local Authority Designated Officer (LADO).[8] The LADO manages allegations against adults who work with children within a local authority area. I was accused of being radicalised, and my journalism of being both 'anti-trans' and 'full of misinformation'. This particular complaint had been triggered by a *Spectator* piece that I had written about Stonewall. It's fair to say that I am not a fan of Stonewall UK, but this is politics: we are allowed to disagree and criticise policy on social media and in the press. But the anonymous sender of the email was having none of that.

> I have become increasingly concerned about the radicalisation of Debbie Hayton, a teacher at... school and her journalism with the Spectator which is both anti trans but also full of misinformation. It must be extremely concerning for parents and children in her class or the

school who maybe [*sic*] trans, gender diverse or LGBT
as she has now extended her attacks onto Stonewall.

In the sixteenth century, the same mentality might have
pursued me for speaking out against the Church. But in
these strange, postmodern times, in some people's minds it
seemed that Stonewall had become the supreme authority
that must not be challenged. The LADO referred the matter
straight back to school. No action was taken by the LADO
because it was blatantly obvious that no pupils were at risk
from my work for the mainstream press. But that did not
preclude action being taken by my school.

Teachers can be dismissed when trust breaks down
between them and the employer. The legal jargon is 'some
other substantial reason'.[9] In my case that never happened –
my employer never wavered in their support for me – but
had the weight of external complaints tipped the scales,
exasperation could easily have seen me out of the door and
out of work. At any time, a change of leadership in the school
could have changed the dynamic completely.

I was on thin ice, but if professionals are not able to
engage in one of the most contentious political disputes of
our time, then the floor will be left to the wealthy, the retired
and the unemployable. As a teacher who was personally
invested in the outcome, I could not let that happen. I had
a point to make, and I was willing to risk my livelihood to
make it.

But then came the T-shirt. It was bold, and it was
designed to challenge the orthodox thinking. I based it on a

Stonewall design. Their slogan 'Trans Women Are Women: Get Over It!' was emblazoned in bold red-and-white type on T-shirts that they sold to the public. I reversed the message to say: 'Trans Women Are Men: Get Over It!', and supplied a local print shop with the digital image. 'It's rather controversial,' I explained.

'Don't worry,' the receptionist replied. 'You should see some of the things that customers would like us to print on a T-shirt.'

There were two parts to the message. The first was what I believed to be the truth. Transwomen like me were adult human males and therefore men. It might not have been to everyone's liking, but I didn't like Stonewall's message either. I reasoned that if Stonewall could make their political statement then I could make mine. But the second part was also a reversal. Stonewall challenged the world to get over the fact that transwomen were women; my focus was inwards. When I had got over the fact that I was still a man – no magic had ever changed my sex – I no longer had to pretend I was anything else. And nor did anyone else. Life is much more secure for me as a result, something I wish for other trans people.

I had several T-shirts printed because I was not the only self-aware transsexual in my network. Others wanted their own. So five went off in the mail and the sixth I wore myself at a July 2019 meeting organised by Woman's Place UK (WPUK) and Fair Play for Women – two organisations that had no doubts about the sex of transwomen. Photos were taken, naturally, and I posted one on social media. I removed it within the day. Not because I had second thoughts about the T-shirt, but because another transsexual had been locked out of Twitter for posting a selfie in which they were wearing their T-shirt. It seemed that there had been a complaint. Someone somewhere had objected, and Twitter ruled that the message – albeit on a T-shirt in a photograph – contravened the terms and conditions of service. Rather than risk a ban myself, I withdrew my tweet.

But once something like that goes out on social media, it rarely comes back quietly. The internet has a habit of remembering, especially when that something has the potential to cause trouble. Copies are downloaded and filed away for later use.

It didn't take long – less than a month, in fact. I picked up the chatter while I was sitting in the departure lounge at Bangkok Airport on 26 July 2019. I had been in Thailand with the NASUWT for an international conference of education unions. There, I moved the draft resolution on LGBTI equality. Serious and pressing issues were discussed: homosexuality is illegal in almost a third of countries across the world, and I was keen to support colleagues who do not enjoy the freedoms we so often take for granted in the UK.[10]

News from the conference was picked up back home. I was criticised robustly by some feminist campaigners – partly for my reported contributions at an LGBTI-equality conference, but partly – I suspect – for wearing a dress in the official photographs. In my defence, it was over thirty degrees. But as my flight home was called, the transgender campaigners started appearing in my notifications. They too were outraged by my attire, but it was not the dress that upset them – they were annoyed by the T-shirt.

Twitter storms are a fascinating insight into human psychology. Outrage is manufactured and the mob forms around it. The participants might not be armed with torches and pitchforks, but the mentality bears a striking resemblance to the witch-hunts of the Middle Ages. Tension builds and onlookers are first drawn in and then they join in. Those hiding behind cloaks of anonymity have nothing to lose. They might fire off only one or two e-missiles but they all hit the target, and anyone else who happens to be tagged in. In this case it was my school and my union. From a standing start, messages were coming in thick and fast. Every time I refreshed my app there were dozens more.

There is no way that anyone can defend themselves against such overwhelming pressure. The best advice is to turn off Twitter and go away. I had no choice: I boarded the aircraft and switched my phone to airplane mode. The internet was mercifully disconnected and the events of the next twelve hours happened without me. I slept well at thirty thousand feet.

By the time I changed planes in Frankfurt, the baiting and public shaming had largely fizzled out. I guess everyone else had to sleep as well. But it had not been forgotten. The outrage percolated more quietly through private groups and private messages. It was not long before my TUC LGBT+ committee colleagues found out. A group of them had already catalogued my supposed transgressions, and filed a complaint. Their letter was directed to Frances O'Grady, the general secretary of the TUC and, for good measure, copied to the general secretary of my own union. A copy came my way in the middle of August, following a call from a senior NASUWT official: 'Debbie, there has been a complaint.'

The letter was almost comical. Laced with faux indignation, the writers painted themselves as victims. 'Dear Frances,' they began. First-name terms, indeed. They continued:

> As Trans women members of the TUC LGBT+ committee we feel compelled to write to you about one of its members: Debbie Hayton. We unequivocally support the right to free speech and a healthy exchange of different viewpoints and political positions. Such discourse, when held in a constructive manner, can only serve to strengthen, not weaken, our movement. We feel, however, that recent actions, words and deeds by Debbie Hayton have moved way beyond healthy discourse and into hate speech. We believe that freedom of speech should never be used as an excuse to spread hate speech.
>
> Debbie has stated, 'Only males can be transwomen, therefore I am male. I'm also an adult. Technically I am a man, and no amount of hormone replacement or surgery will actually change that… This is true for all trans women whether we like it or not.'[11]
>
> In making this inflammatory statement Debbie Hayton is engaging in the basest biological reductionism, and supremacist theorising. Debbie is positing that the only claim to authentic womanhood is by cis women, and thereby denigrating Transwomen as not being honest

to themselves or about themselves. This is summed up when she writes: 'Trans people have to live in the real world and the key evidence is not what's in our heads but what's between our legs…'[12]

With these words Debbie Hayton not only runs counter to the modern understanding of gender identity…

It seemed that unequivocally supporting the rights of free speech did not extend to the defence of biological reality. I'm happy for anyone to disagree with me, but clearly my graciousness in debate was not reciprocated. But if they didn't want to debate with me, they could have turned to the democratic process. I was elected to the committee each year. Yes, I had been returned unopposed, though it was to an unpaid position that involved long and sometimes intricate committee meetings. It was hardly glamorous work, but all they needed to do was find another candidate. The electorate were the delegates to the TUC LGBT+ conference and, after the events of July 2018, they would probably have picked a Tory before me.

But instead, the letter writers turned to veiled threats. Five paragraphs later, they concluded:

We are all active members of the Trans community, and the LGBT+ movement, and we know that eyes are now firmly focused on the TUC and how it deals with this situation. We call on the TUC to act decisively and in positive support of Trans and non-binary identities in this matter as a matter of urgency.

It seemed that the TUC acted by pestering my own union. I am still not sure what the letter writers expected the TUC or the NASUWT to do, but they were clearly not satisfied. That first letter of complaint had been signed by three members of the committee – all transwomen. A subsequent letter was attributed to nine more, including the chair of the TUC LGBT+ committee herself. As well as the T-shirt, they took umbrage with a piece I had just written for the *Morning Star*.[13] A majority of committee members plus the supposedly impartial chair now accused me of hate speech. In this latest missive, Frances O'Grady was told:

> Most recently (July 2019) Debbie Hayton posted a picture of herself online wearing a T shirt with the slogan, 'Transwomen are Men. Get over it' and (October 2019) tweeted a link to her article for the Morning Star with the summary 'Trans women are biologically male – in fact being male is the sole qualifying criteria [*sic*] to be a trans woman – and women are biologically female. Male people are not female people and therefore trans women are not women. Those are the facts.'[14]
>
> These actions, we believe, moves [*sic*] from debate into hate speech that should not be tolerated within the TUC.

My logical and reasonable arguments might have been grounded in science but, like religious zealots, my persecutors were having none of it. 'Hate speech!' they shrieked. Their letter continued:

We fully support the letter of complaint from the Trans women on our Committee sent to you on 12/08/19 and ask that you deal with their concerns with the utmost seriousness. Large sections of the LGBT+ community are incensed at the words and deeds of Debbie Hayton, and the reputation and trust in the TUC as an inclusive organisation is [*sic*] being tarnished.

The intimidation reached levels beyond even my previous experience. It was far worse than any Twitter storm: fellow committee members – erstwhile friends, even – were pleading with the general secretary of the TUC to deal with me for hate speech. In my view I had merely spoken truth and reality, but it would have been impossible to defend myself alone from what seemed to me to be an angry mob that outnumbered me twelve to one. Had it not been for the support of the NASUWT I may have crumbled. Unions exist to protect their members and the NASUWT defended me. The complaints were repudiated, and it was pointed out – quite rightly – that there were no procedures to discipline individual elected committee members in any case.

But there were procedures in place to regulate the conduct of TUC meetings. The next committee meeting was looming. Twitter storms and letter-writing campaigns are nasty, but meetings are real life. The chair and a majority of members had accused me of hate speech. Without a hint of irony, they had also complained about not feeling safe. From what? The truth, that men cannot become women? There were certainly more of them than there was of me. I travelled to London with foreboding. It would be the last physical meeting of the full TUC LGBT+ committee that I would ever attend, and it was a meeting like no other that I have experienced before or since.

7

APOSTASY AND EXCLUSION

Until COVID-19 locked the nation down in March 2020, the TUC LGBT+ committee convened physically at Congress House itself, a 1950s building on Great Russell Street, close to the British Museum in central London. The date – 17 October 2019 – had been in my diary well before the furore blew up over my T-shirt. When the calendar of meetings was drawn up, everyone expected yet another routine committee meeting, the first in the cycle where we usually evaluated the recent conference. After the drama of 2018, I had kept my head well down in 2019 before being re-elected to the committee unopposed.

I did wonder whether there might be some kind of protest on the pavement, but everything was quiet when I arrived shortly before the meeting began. The receptionist guided me to the usual meeting room; despite the fury that had been directed my way, I had a job to do. I had been elected to receive reports from TUC officials and, together with my colleagues, verify that conference resolutions were being progressed. As a member of the NASUWT I also reported back to my own union's officials after every meeting. So, I assembled my papers, unpacked my laptop, grabbed a coffee and settled down to work. Half a dozen or so committee members were already sitting around the big table, and others arrived later. A colleague from my own union – there were two elected representatives from the NASUWT present that day – sat next to me. I knew I had his support, but the atmosphere in the room was icy and the glances that came my way were distinctly frosty. I ignored them and focused on the agenda. Item 7 was the chair's report, which ran to several points. Point 6 needed no explanation: 'Complaint to the TUC'.

The meeting began with eighteen members present; together we represented fourteen different unions. Two TUC officials – members of staff at Congress House – sat alongside the committee chair. Did they have a plan to avoid World War Three, I wondered? I reckoned that we would get to item 7, point 6 in about half an hour. We co-opted a nominee into a vacant seat and agreed the minutes from last time, and we were into the report from the chair. Several routine points came and went, but all minds were focused on point 6. When the moment arrived, the chair announced that she had attended a complaint meeting on 3 October, and there was to be no discussion in committee. With barely a pause of breath, she moved straight on to point 7 in her report: reform of the Gender Recognition Act.

The government had failed to introduce self-ID – 'wimped out', according to one voice around the table. Committee decided that it needed to make a response. Personally, I was delighted, but these meetings had never been a safe environment for me to express my reservations about a policy based on what I saw to be no more than feelings. That day, I knew I really did need to keep my own counsel. A draft statement was circulated for discussion. 'Make it clear that we welcomed the consultation,' one colleague suggested. Minor points of detail were suggested: 'I propose an amendment to paragraph 3. Remove the word *renew* and insert the word *continue*.' It was hardly an earth-shattering debate, but it was only the calm before the storm. What followed was a tempest.

If the official plan had been to avoid all discussion of The Complaint, my colleague from the National Education Union (NEU) had other ideas. Perhaps it was as well that she was on the other side of the table – she appeared to be furious. 'Going back to point 6, I have seen certain things on social media...' She insisted that her feelings be put on record, and continued: 'It goes against the principles of this committee, and I feel uncomfortable on this committee.' Her comments were barbed and directed directly at me. She added: 'As a member of an education union there are other education unions involved and there is a safeguarding issue here.'

The NEU representative was cut off quickly by one of the TUC officials, who remarked that 'people have referenced the complaint'. The official insisted that 'there is a process underway, and it is not appropriate that there is any further discussion regarding the complaint'. In case anyone had not heard the first time, she repeated: 'There is a formal process underway, and people will be heard.'

That was the first I had heard about a formal process. I would learn more about it in the weeks to come, but, for now, I suddenly felt very vulnerable on a committee where more than half the members – including the chair – had accused me of hate speech. I was in a minority, and I feared for my safety. But the majority saw things in a completely different light. The member representing Prospect entered the fray and demanded action on safeguarding: 'There has been a shortfall in the duty of care. We are volunteers, and we are not being protected. The TUC should have dealt with this issue quicker.'

Was she really demanding to be kept safe from me? There were at least twelve of them and only one of me. By now it was clear that the instruction not to discuss the complaint had been in vain: committee members demanded answers.

'What is the complaint procedure? What is the mechanism?'

The TUC official tried valiantly to correct the misinformation – she explained that committee members were not volunteers, but representatives of their trade unions – and pleaded for no further discussion about the complaint. Otherwise, 'the meeting will be halted.'

Members continued to press for information. From where I was sitting it felt as if they had now smelled blood – my blood – and they were demanding to know the method of execution: 'We want to know the process; we couldn't find anything in writing.'

After the official once again threatened to stop the meeting, the chair muddied the waters. She suggested that the member wasn't asking about the complaint – which had been forbidden – but the process. The official once again demanded that we return to the agenda, or the meeting really would be halted. But there was fat chance of getting back to business. Emotion had overcome reason: committee members demanded action. But, like a self-righteous mob, they did not see themselves as persecutors – they were the victims.

The Prospect rep who had been concerned about the shortfall in the duty of care – to her, presumably – went back to the committee statement that we were supposed to be discussing, and turned it into a new line of attack: 'If we cannot all support that statement on GRA reform, why is anyone here?'

The TUC official resorted to the terms of reference, telling everyone that this was an *advisory* committee. We were reminded that we could advise the TUC General Council to issue a statement to protest the inaction of the government on GRA reform, but the LGBT+ committee did not make policy.

The atmosphere in the room was already angry, as the objections of female committee members had been rebuffed by the female official. But, so far, the attack was from women. What motivated them I could only guess. Did they want to be kind? In which case, to whom? It certainly wasn't me. Or did they want to be seen as good people? Defending a group that they perceived to be oppressed and marginalised ticked that box. But my presence in that room turned them from rescuers into persecutors – the only person being oppressed and marginalised that day was me. I dared not even open my mouth.

I knew exactly what motivated the transwomen, though. I understand transwomen because I am one. We are not women, and sometimes we behave quite differently from women. There were three transwomen in the room besides me. So far, they had let the women do the talking, but finally one of them had had enough. It was Clicky Heels from last year's TUC LGBT+ conference – who had since been elected to the committee. But we were not interrupted by a point of order; this time there was an outburst of raw fury:

'I stood up at Trans Pride Brighton and told them that the TUC's five and a half million were behind the reforms. Now I feel like a charlatan. The wider trans community is outraged and shaking its head in disbelief.'

With that, Clicky Heels stood up, slammed a hand into the wall, and stormed out of the meeting. As the crash reverberated around the room, it seemed that the motivation was neither emancipation nor liberation – these people were driven by power. Some transwomen, perhaps with insignificant histories, had found that after coming out as transgender they could set the agenda. They could stand on platforms, assume the support of millions of working people, and use it to impose their will on society. And woe betide anyone who dared to stand in their way.

The chair suggested a ten-minute break. She left the room along with most of the committee. Both officials followed. I stayed with my NASUWT colleague and a handful of others. Nobody among this remnant had signed a complaint, and neither had they contributed to the most recent debate. So, while there was no articulated support for me in the room, I suspected that the committee was not of one mind in feeding me to the wolves. I could only speculate on the discussions that took place in the corridor, so I got on with the job and prepared my committee report for the NASUWT – a document that was turning out to be one like no other.

As I typed up my notes, committee members began to return. Clicky Heels, however, was absent. Perhaps too traumatised by their own impotence to come back into the room, I mused. I had stood my ground; I was going nowhere. The chair came back midway through an animated conversation with one of the officials. 'I am the chair of this committee,' she snarled.

Then, just over an hour into business that had been scheduled to run all day, the chair briefly reconvened the meeting to announce:

'Because someone has had to leave the meeting because they feel unsafe, we cannot continue with the meeting. Because one person feels unsafe.'

Safety had also become a weapon of the powerful, it seems. Along with violence, of course. I grimaced at the irony. The only committee member who had been violent was the one who now claimed to feel unsafe. The TUC official tried to gloss over the chair's outrageous claim. She agreed with the chair that it was not right to continue the meeting but added: 'It is not a safe place for people.' 'People', being plural, presumably included me. But the chair was having none of that. She insisted that the meeting was not safe for Clicky Heels.

At that point, the TUC officials rose from their seats and walked straight out of the room. I was suddenly left in the company of my detractors. There was, for a moment, stunned silence. If any previous TUC meeting had ever been halted in such a dramatic fashion, we didn't know about it. The NEU representative moaned that our next meeting was 'not until February, and we have a lot of business to get through'. She had been the one who 'had seen things on social media' and effectively set light to the meeting. Any sense of irony was lost in the tension.

The TUC officials reappeared to shoo us out of Congress House. 'We will be in touch with unions. The TUC is committed to this committee. The next scheduled meeting is in February. This meeting is now over.' At that point we were all instructed to leave the building because the TUC was unable to guarantee our safety. The officials again left the room, again leaving me in the company of some people who had zero regard for my safety. But I was determined not to leave the room first.

After what felt like an age, colleagues began to leave. There were mutterings about a group photo. That was the first I had heard about that. I followed them out to try to see what they had planned. My NASUWT colleague was as clueless as me. We compared notes as we headed for the front door. Something was definitely happening on the steps outside Congress House. Colleagues were partially disrobing to reveal black T-shirts that declared 'Trans Women Are Women: Get Over It!'

The officials reappeared once more and offered me a back door out. I declined; this was my committee and they appeared to be setting up for a photo stunt outside the home of trade unionism in Great Britain. I wanted to see what was happening so I stood prominently by the front door. If any photo was taken now, I would be in the back of it. The discomfort and disarray among the group was palpable, and not because it had begun to drizzle. The committee chair announced that they would reconvene in a nearby pub. I was clearly not invited, and I made my way home alone. The group photo was posted on social media at 7.20 p.m.[1] The backdrop was the British Museum. Fifteen members of the TUC LGBT+ committee – all decked out in those black T-shirts – looked into the camera with their fists raised.

It had been a surreal day: a routine TUC business meeting had descended into chaos. I had faced bullying, intimidation and abuse. A dozen or more trade union representatives – my colleagues – had accused me of hate speech and making another transwoman feel 'unsafe'. It was not me who had unleashed my frustration on a wall, but there was no hope of defending myself in that particular kangaroo court. In their minds I was guilty as charged.

If two letters of complaint were not enough, they were followed by a third epistle a week after the shenanigans at Congress House. This time my colleagues cited a judgement made by Twitter. My account had been locked after I had commented wryly on the antics of another transgender campaigner. This particular transwoman had posted a selfie of themselves dancing in the women's toilets. I retorted:

I have lots of female friends. None has ever posted a video of themselves in the toilets. I have fewer trans friends but you are not the first to do so (though I concede you are the first dancer). I wonder if it's male pattern behaviour: marking out and claiming territory?

According to Twitter, that amounted to 'hateful conduct' and I was banned from posting for seven days. My appeal was ignored, and so I was forced to delete the tweet and take the strike. The complainants reported these developments in that third letter to the TUC. They wrote:

Debbie's twitter account has been suspended for seven days because of substantiated claims that it contains such discriminatory and inflammatory language.

In previous communications we have brought to your attention numerous examples of hate speech and actions perpetrated by Dr Hayton, yet you still see it as plausible that other trans women (in particular) and non-binary people on the TUC LGBT+ committee should attend its meetings with Debbie present.

It is also worth noting that Dr Hayton has also tweeted support for the new LGB Alliance: an openly anti-trans organisation that aims to split the LGBT+ community and targets Stonewall in particular. We have to ask, how such support is consistent with the aims and policy of the TUC in general and the TUC LGBT+ committee in particular?

Not only were my ideas condemned as heresy, but I had also now criticised Stonewall. When I first joined the TUC LGBT+ committee in 2015, Stonewall was treated with suspicion. While we represented workers, Stonewall collected payment from their bosses. But by 2019, this organisation was seemingly beyond reproach. If gender identity ideology had been a religion, trans people would be the priestly class and Stonewall perhaps the Church itself. In this corner of the trade union movement at least, the class struggle had been eclipsed by quasi-religious dogma, and in only four years. With the confidence of modern-day witchfinders, they added:

> Constantly we are told that such expressions are matters of individual opinion and not the purview of the TUC. Hate speech is not a matter of expressing an opinion in the spirit of debate: it is hate speech.
>
> These are very dangerous and scary times for many Trans people as moderate women who are Trans [sic] inclusive are attacked and Stonewall is targeted… We place our trust in you to do what is right.

I shuddered to think what they might have had in mind. As it was, I was invited to attend an investigation meeting at Congress House. After twenty years as a union rep, I knew all about investigation meetings. I had attended many, but every time to advise the member who was being investigated. For the first time in my career, it was me under the spotlight. I returned to Congress House one Tuesday afternoon in November 2019 to answer questions. I entered the building for the first time since that aborted meeting in a state of nervous apprehension.

Thankfully, I was not alone. I was represented in the meeting by a senior NASUWT official – someone from my own union. I was convinced that I had done nothing wrong, and I had certainly not broken any rules because there were none to break. I had been assured of that – I was an elected representative, and not a paid employee. We listened carefully as the investigating officer set out the case. She referred to the three letters in turn. By now, I knew the contents by heart.

What followed was straight from the NASUWT training manual for school representatives – whenever a member is facing an investigation, always focus on the policy. If the employer isn't following policy, there may not even be a case to answer. My representative was insistent: 'What rule do the complainants think that Debbie might have broken?'

The investigating officer squirmed. 'There is no rule' – adding that this was an informal process to find out what has happened.

My representative asserted – correctly – that if this was merely an 'informal process' then we were not required to attend any meetings, and we certainly did not need to respond to any questions. But since we are all together, he added: 'Debbie might like to say how she feels.' He pointed out that I had been harassed, intimidated, marginalised and ultimately excluded from a committee photo, merely for having a different opinion. After some closing pleasantries – we all knew each other, after all – I left for home and heard no more about any TUC processes, informal or otherwise.

Whatever happened next between the TUC and the complainants was their business, but Clicky Heels was clearly not satisfied, and took to Twitter to call for my resignation: 'As the other trans member of the TUC LGBT+ committee I am totally appalled by your behaviour towards the trans community and the hurt it is causing. Please do the decent thing and resign from the committee.' The attached image showed me wearing my 'Transwomen Are Men' T-shirt.

I didn't appreciate the comments, but ignoring them was a better strategy than engaging in an unedifying public spat. But the series of late-night tweets that followed were directed at my union, the Labour Party (of which I was a member) and anybody, it seemed, who might have been able to take action against me. Finally, the Metropolitan Police was alerted: '@metpoliceuk Hi, this person wore this transphobic T-shirt in Central London in July. Why was nothing done about it?'

Unlike me, the Met responded publicly: 'Hi, was this reported at the time? If not, it can be reported here.'[2] The police added a link to an online form. Whether anything was ever reported I do not know. I had not broken any rules, nor had I transgressed the law. It is not illegal in the UK to hold the opinion that transwomen are men – not yet, anyway. But in the weeks that followed, I struggled to sleep easily at night.

Would I be required to help the police with their enquiries at six o'clock the following morning?

The next committee meeting, in February 2020, was carefully stage-managed. There was no gathering of the full committee. Instead, we were divided among several sub-committees, which were kept apart in the building. I didn't see any of the complainants, and they didn't see me. Then, in March 2020, we were locked down with the rest of the UK and our meetings were moved online for the rest of the year. There was no TUC LGBT+ conference in July 2020 – COVID-19 precautions made that impossible – so the trade unions sent in block votes to elect committee members for the following year. I was not returned, and my dissenting ideas were shut out. The complaints and the TUC investigation achieved nothing: in the end I was removed by the democratic process.

My experience did, however, reveal the impact of an ideology that tolerates no dissent when it establishes itself within an organisation. The trade union movement was a prime example of institutional capture. I would be astonished if trade union leaders had forgotten how to distinguish men and women or thought that the difference did not matter. But for too many it did not seem to matter enough when political capital was at stake. With big battles to be won over pay and conditions of employment, why pick a fight over transgender inclusion? The equalities streams were active within trade unions and they provided a ready source of activists. If the potential for abusive men to take advantage of self-identification registered with union leaderships, then

I can only assume that they thought that maybe nothing sufficiently bad would happen before it all blew over.

Equalities was certainly a fertile ground for future activism. I was but one example. Having been nurtured in the equalities sector, I now invested my time and energy representing my members in the workplace and on the NASUWT's National Executive. The world was changing more rapidly than anyone could have imagined before COVID-19 broke into the news agenda at the start of 2020. My profession worked a miracle during the lockdowns that followed. Teachers who had been oblivious to online teaching methods retrained themselves in four days flat. On Wednesday, 19 March 2020, the prime minister announced to the nation that schools would close to most pupils at the end of the week. The following Monday, along with many thousands of my colleagues, I sat in front of my webcam with hastily redesigned resources and taught my pupils remotely. But we received little in the way of thanks. Pay erosion continued, while some school leaders – perhaps under huge pressure themselves – engaged in what the union described as 'adverse management practices'. I continued to support members in dispute with their schools, leading negotiations with their employers.

Dispute talks and members' meetings all moved online. That was another very new experience – we negotiate with far more than words. But that was easy by comparison to what followed a session with the employer. When I took an offer back to members, I needed to gauge their collective response. A few members might speak up – some vociferously – but, to read the room, I needed to understand body language. How many members are hanging on the words of the speaker, and how many are more interested in their phones? That peripheral vision is useless when each member is represented by a little black rectangle on a computer monitor. But we managed; we even held virtual picket lines.

My term on the National Executive, and consequently my role as a negotiator, ended in July 2021. Stephanie had secured a new job in Bristol, so – after more than two decades in the Midlands – we relocated to the south-west of England. NEMs represented a geographical district – in my case the West Midlands urban area that stretched from Wolverhampton to Coventry. As union work reverted to what we had always known – real, physical meetings in workplaces – someone local was needed. So I informed my colleagues that I would not seek re-election as their NEM; my role drew to a close at the end of my term of office.

Instead, I decided to run for national president. The NASUWT had supported me unstintingly throughout my trials and tribulations at the TUC: I could not have asked for better representation. I had the necessary skills and experience – I was a proven negotiator and I had chaired TUC conferences. I also had the support of colleagues, a not insignificant detail in a democratic organisation.

The elected office to which I aspired was a four-year term as a 'national officer'. The presidential year is actually year three of four. The four officers on the presidential rotation, along with the honorary treasurer, are the most senior lay roles in a union with almost 300,000 members. Twice I campaigned for the post. The first time I finished second out of five in a national ballot of members. I congratulated the victor and went back to my supporters to try again. I secured their nominations a second time and, just before Christmas 2021, I was elected. Nowhere in my campaign literature did I trumpet the fact that I was trans; it just didn't seem important. I was simply a trade unionist who could do the job well. By that time my national profile was such that many members did know, but they chose me nevertheless. My election exemplified how far trans people had come in the UK. The rights that really mattered – being allowed to get on with life – were secure. Being transsexual was not an issue in my election as president, nor has it been in my work as a teacher. Trans rights are indeed human rights because trans people are human people.

Unfortunately, things did not work out as I had hoped at the start of 2022. Had I been a more private individual – or had I not said so much about the need to respect biological reality – then I would likely have taken office in April of that year, and would have been looking forward to becoming national president in 2024. But I had said what I thought was right, rather than what was politically advantageous. Transwomen are not women, because we are the opposite sex to women. Others might not like to hear that – and I have suffered harassment, intimidation and abuse as a result – but, ultimately, I could not deny the truth.

It was not just me who suffered. Complaints continued to be made to both the union and my school. Both stood firm, and I remain grateful to both organisations for not caving in to bullying. Apart from that ridiculous investigation by the TUC, no disciplinary action was ever taken against me. How could it? I had done nothing to warrant it – it is not an offence to upset third parties by uttering scientific truths that they do not wish to hear. But the prospect of me becoming a national officer created a political dynamic that ultimately dashed my hopes.

Two weeks before I was due to take office, the NASUWT published a position statement on trans rights.[3] I was neither consulted nor informed before it hit the website. It began: 'The NASUWT fully supports trans workers' rights and welcomes the increased visibility and empowerment of trans and non-binary people in society.' I had no argument with that, though I might have pointed out that surely everyone is non-binary. But it continued:

> We are committed to campaign for a simplified, free, statutory gender-recognition process based on self-declaration and to support rights for gender non-binary people at work and in wider society.
>
> The Union supports the right of all women (including trans women) to safe spaces and the continuation of monitoring that can help identify discrimination and harassment against women and men.

That text had been lifted straight from Motion 41, which the NASUWT had supported at the TUC Congress in 2018. Four years after I had argued unsuccessfully for the union to oppose what I considered to be dangerous nonsense, those words had come back to bite. Self-declaration had – in my view – caused problems for trans people, certainly not made our lives easier. In the 2016 blog piece in which I had first voiced my concerns, I predicted that 'transwomen in particular may find that goodwill is replaced by suspicion should abusive men spot an opportunity to exploit women's spaces and protections'.[4] I took no pleasure in sensing that I had been right.

If legal gender recognition can be claimed by anyone, it is available to everyone and the consequences are all too predictable. If women's 'safe spaces' must be opened up to transwomen, then they must include any man who chooses to identify in that way. They are no longer single-sex spaces by definition. I knew this, and I suspect that others in the union knew it. The position statement was not actually policy – that would need to have been agreed by the NASUWT annual conference – but it was official and there was no prospect of getting it removed.

As soon as I saw it I knew what I must do. My heart sank. I could try to ignore the statement, but as president – a transsexual president, indeed – I would likely face questions: 'What is your view on the union's position on trans rights, Debbie?' Perhaps I could claim a Damascene conversion to self-identification and the belief that transwomen are somehow women, but I believed no such thing. Besides, my credibility as a campaigner would be torn to shreds. I might try to fudge the question, but I'd seen too many politicians tie themselves up in knots. It's tiring, exasperating and ulti-mately futile – in the end they upset everyone. Or I could be honest and explain how I was personally opposed to a statement that ultimately harmed trans rights by undermining the trust and confidence that underpin the acceptance of trans people in society. But that would make my position as president untenable. I would be seen to undermine a position statement on what might be the most politically contentious issue of our time.

So, two weeks before I was due to take office, I offered my resignation to the general secretary and walked away from the opportunity to lead my union. I was upset and filled with regret – but I knew that the alternative would be worse. I would have been distraught had I compromised my own principles; instead, I remained free to campaign for what I thought was right.

Some people agree with me; others don't. But if we are to formulate good policy then all voices must surely be heard, and all ideas tested, to reach agreements that accommodate everybody's needs. That, however, will require openness and a willingness to make ourselves vulnerable to others. Too few people – it seems – are willing to do that. The urge to 'keep safe' is not without consequences.

While most of the opposition I face still comes from trans people and their allies, an increasing proportion comes from women defending their right to single-sex spaces. Taking the NASUWT position statement as one example, they have just cause. How can women maintain single-sex spaces when even my own union argues that those spaces should be open to members of both sexes? Naive approaches – from well-meaning people, perhaps – have fuelled uncertainty and undermined the confidence people had in structures and organisations. The result is an increasingly polarised dispute that seems to get ever more toxic with no winners in sight. We can argue about how we got here, but the far more important question is: how do we get out of the mess?

8

TERF ISLAND: BRITAIN AGAINST THE WORLD

ARGUABLY the mess started in the 1960s when those American psychiatrists invented the concept of gender identity and used it to label individuals gripped by certain psychological disorders. Why have a disorder – something wrong with you that needs treating – when you can have an identity? But it was after Yogyakarta, in 2006, that the concept was shoehorned into policy along with sexual orientation. The acronym SOGI (Sexual Orientation and Gender Identity) was born, and it became a key human rights campaign, and – according to the 'Dentons document' – something not only for adults.[1]

The activists' tactics were transparently opaque, but something remarkable happened when attention turned to the UK. Elsewhere governments and administrations had caved in and both gender identity and self-ID had become enshrined in law. Initially, it seemed that the UK would follow. Even before legislation was passed, policymakers had got themselves 'ahead of the government', to use the language of the 'Dentons document'. When even the prison service placed rapists and their male genitalia in women's jails, activists could argue with a straight face that legal self-ID was merely a tidying-up operation. Initially, everything went to plan. Following the select committee report on transgender equality, the UK government set out its plans for self-ID.[2] Trying to play down the issue, the minister for women and equalities said: 'What we want to try to do is streamline the process, make it easier, demedicalise it and make it less intrusive.'[3]

But this time there was organised resistance, and it emerged from the same trade union movement in which I had felt harassed, intimidated and abused. Woman's Place UK (WPUK) was founded in September 2017 by Judith Green, Ruth Serwotka and Kiri Tunks.[4] The three were well-known trade unionists. Tunks would go on to serve as joint president of the NEU, while Serwotka was married to the general secretary of the PCS. They were as far from that caricature of the right-wing reactionary conservative as it is possible to imagine. While they were routinely attacked as TERFs – originally 'trans-exclusionary radical feminists', but more latterly a slur hurled at anyone who knows the difference between women and transwomen – they campaigned to uphold the rights of women. Particularly in the face of the likely consequences of that streamlining process.

Their new organisation – with its distinctive yellow-and-black branding – was born shortly after Maria MacLachlan was assaulted by a transgender activist in Hyde Park.[5]

MacLachlan was there to attend a meeting organised by another group to discuss the prospect of self-ID, and the potential consequences for women's rights. The original venue had cancelled following pressure from activists, so MacLachlan and others were advised to meet at Speakers' Corner, in Hyde Park. There they would be given directions to a secret replacement venue. The fact that such measures needed to be adopted by a women's group in 2017 should give everyone pause for thought, but that evening the activists went further than mere threats. 'When TERFs attack, we fight back,' they chanted. Then, twenty-six-year-old Tara Wolf – a self-declared 'trans woman' – grabbed at MacLachlan's camera, punched her and assaulted her. The video evidence was compelling: Wolf was convicted and ordered to pay £430 in fines and costs.[6]

It must have been clear to anyone who had thought about it that if any man can self-declare himself to be a woman for all legal purposes then women's boundaries become meaningless, but too few people were thinking. WPUK held meetings – real-life events in church halls and community centres up and down the country – where speakers would bring the message to local people. Shockingly, the 'When TERFs attack, we fight back' brigade would picket their meetings and intimidate ordinary women – some old enough to be their grandmothers.

The meetings themselves were never single-sex events: men were very welcome. Kevin Courtney, joint general secretary of the NEU – Tunks's own union – went to a meeting in Brighton. He reported his observations on social media: 'I decided to come and see what the [WPUK] meeting was all about tonight. The protestors outside are banging on the windows so loud that you can't hear yourself think inside. That can't be the right way to deal with the issue.'[7] As the meeting ended, he added: 'I'm very pleased to have come. I've heard opinions that the protestors wouldn't agree with. I haven't heard any hate speech.'[8]

Presumably, he meant that he heard no hate speech inside the building. WPUK attracted hateful responses from outside their meetings, simply because they campaigned for the rights of women to define their sex. The *Morning Star* reported that one woman was doused in water as she entered, while a young PhD student was reduced to tears and missed most of the subsequent meeting because the 'terrifying' experience brought on a panic attack.[9]

Those protestors would have been better advised to go inside and listen politely to what was said from the platform. Socialist feminist campaigner Dani Ahrens told the meeting: 'I'm not an enemy of trans people and nothing I have said tonight is an attempt to deny anyone's rights.' It was the increasingly militant lobby stationed outside that seemed intent on trampling over the rights of others.

The biggest irony for me was that WPUK not only welcomed transsexuals to their meetings, but also platformed two of us on multiple occasions. I spoke at three meetings in 2018, while Kristina Harrison – a paramedic who had transitioned many years previously – addressed three more. Yes, we both opposed self-ID, and our support for WPUK's aims was genuine, but the group faced criticism as a result. However, from my perspective I observed an organisation focused on the rights of women, not the marginalisation of trans people. Like good trade unionists, WPUK developed sound policy statements that respected everyone's rights. It was an approach that won them a large following.

WPUK was not alone in the campaign against self-ID. Fair Play for Women took a meticulous approach to policy – and policy failings – among organisations and governing bodies that were already so far ahead of the law that their policies did not comply with current legislation.[10] Transgender Trend foresaw the devastating impact on children when they are effectively told a huge lie: that they are able to choose whether they grow up to be a woman or a man.[11]

In time, others would join them. In October 2020, a group of campaigners including Maya Forstater launched the organisation Sex Matters.[12] Forstater had lost her job with the European arm of the think tank Center for Global Development (CGD) after pointing out on social media something that everyone once knew to be true – that people cannot change their biological sex. At her first employment tribunal in December 2019, judge James Tayler ruled that Forstater's approach was 'not worthy of respect in a democratic society'.[13] That judgment was overturned on appeal, but not before author J. K. Rowling came out strongly in support of Forstater. In April 2022, journalist Helen Joyce, author of *Trans: When Ideology Meets Reality*, a best-selling account of the transgender phenomenon published in July 2021, joined the organisation as its director of advocacy.[14]

North of the border, the Scottish government pursued self-ID with enthusiasm. Gender recognition is a 'devolved matter', so the Scottish parliament in Edinburgh could pass legislation to uncouple Scottish law from that of the rest of the UK. There were multiple consultations and much controversy. If the Scottish government thought that they might sneak this legislation in under the radar, they were in for a shock.

From 2018, For Women Scotland drew in huge grassroots support to oppose the government bill; at the same time, the painstaking work of Dr Kath Murray, Dr Lucy Hunter Blackburn and Lisa Mackenzie – known collectively as Murray Blackburn Mackenzie (MBM) – did what government officials failed to do.[15] They showed that the proposed Gender Recognition Reform Bill (Scotland) would fall foul of the Equality Act 2010 – UK-wide legislation that had certainly not been devolved.

The Equality Act has always sat uneasily alongside the 2004 Gender Recognition Act. The former protected sex, without properly defining the word. Biology was absent when sex was defined in the following terms: 'a reference to a person who has a particular protected characteristic is a reference to a man or to a woman.'[16]

Perhaps those who drafted the Equality Act never imagined the potential for future controversy over what it means to be a man or a woman. Yes, we had always known the difference, but, a decade later, many now seemed ashamed to remember it. In February 2023 – just before she stood down as Scottish first minister – Nicola Sturgeon prevaricated when asked if Isla Bryson, a fully intact male rapist, was a man or a woman: 'She regards herself as a woman. I regard the individual as a rapist,' was the closest Sturgeon came to clarifying her position.[17]

The earlier GRA had effectively created the concept of 'legal sex'. Despite all the talk of gender in that piece of legislation and elsewhere, the objective category is sex, and it is sex – not gender – that is recorded on birth certificates. According to section 9 of the GRA: 'the person's gender becomes for all purposes the acquired gender (so that, if the acquired gender is the male gender, the person's sex becomes that of a man and, if it is the female gender, the person's sex becomes that of a woman).'[18]

The GRA may not have had the power to change biological sex – that really would be magic – but it certainly appeared to change someone's legal sex, and 'for all purposes'. Confusingly, however, there were exceptions. A woman could not use a GRC to take a hereditary peerage from her younger brother, for example, and nor would the younger brother lose it if he transitioned the other way.[19] There was also an opt-out clause for clergy should they be asked to solemnise a marriage involving someone with a GRC.[20]

But what really mattered was the impact of a GRC on single-sex exceptions permitted by the Equality Act.[21] Did the Equality Act refer to *biological* men and women, or *legal* men and women? It didn't say, and, for around 6,000 people in the UK who already had a GRC, it really mattered. The self-ID bill proposed for Scotland might have increased that number significantly – the Scottish government estimated that the number of GRCs issued in Scotland would

rise from around thirty to between 250 and 300 per year.²²
At the same time the process would be available to a wider
group of people.

The question remained unanswered as the self-ID Gender
Recognition Reform Bill made its way through the Scottish
parliament. Then, on 13 December 2022 – just one week
before the final debate and vote – the Haldane judgment
was handed down in the Edinburgh Court of Session.²³
For Women Scotland had petitioned Lady Haldane to
rule on a different piece of legislation entirely. The Gender
Representation on Public Boards (Scotland) Act 2018 set out
the objective that 50 per cent of the non-executive members
on public boards should be women.²⁴ But were those biological women, or legal women? The 2018 Act, incidentally,
had suggested something else entirely:

> 'woman' includes a person who has the protected char-
> acteristic of gender reassignment (within the meaning
> of section 7 of the Equality Act 2010) if, and only if, the
> person is living as a woman and is proposing to undergo,
> is undergoing or has undergone a process (or part of a
> process) for the purpose of becoming female.²⁵

The Act failed to explain what it meant to 'live as a woman' –
a shortcoming it shared with the GRA – but then muddied
the waters even further. What sort of process could possibly
turn a male human being into a female human being? There
was no clue in the legislation, so For Women Scotland was
right to ask questions. But Lady Haldane's answer was

probably not what they were looking for. She ruled that unless it was clear that sex meant biological sex, then legal sex took precedence:

> I conclude that in this context, which is the meaning of sex for the purposes of the 2010 Act, 'sex' is not limited to biological or birth sex, but includes those in possession of a GRC obtained in accordance with the 2004 Act stating their acquired gender, and thus their sex.[26]

However, there was at least clarity. It now seemed that a GRC changed someone's legal sex for Equality Act purposes. A service provider who claimed a single-sex exception in order to provide a single-sex service for women would thus be required to include transwomen who had been issued with a GRC. Clearly, if the new Scottish Gender Recognition Reform Bill was passed, there would be material change in the number of GRCs issued – and to whom they could be issued (sixteen- and seventeen-year-olds were included, for starters). There would therefore be a material impact on the Equality Act. But since the Equality Act is 'reserved legislation' – the responsibility of the UK Parliament in London – there was now the very real prospect of a constitutional crisis.

The Scottish government charged ahead with their self-ID legislation regardless. The final debates were scheduled for the week before Christmas. Sittings went on until the early hours – certainly not the normal practice for the supposedly 'family-friendly' Scottish parliament – as over a hundred amendments were considered, and mostly struck down.[27] Finally, on 22 December 2022, the bill was passed by 86 votes to 39.

That might have been the end of the parliamentary session, but it was not the end of the matter. The Scottish government had been keen to draw parallels with Ireland. There, self-ID legislation had been sneaked through in 2015. The Dentons document cited the outcome as a case study:

> The legislation went under the radar in Ireland because marriage equality was gaining the most focus. In a way, this was helpful according to the activists, because it meant that they were able to focus on persuading politicians that the change was necessary. This is a common technique that we have seen in many of the successful campaigns, and it was very effective in Ireland.[28]

The Scottish public had been alerted to the problems of self-ID, including the disturbing reports from Limerick women's prison in the south-west of Ireland. Transgender-identified male prisoners were being held there. One had been convicted of ten counts of sexual assault and one count of cruelty against a child.[29] 'The Irish Prison Service must accept all prisoners into custody into whatever prison a judge orders,' the minister for justice said in response to a parliamentary question.[30]

The chair of the Irish Law Society's Criminal Law Committee explained:

> The law that was enacted in 2015 did not envisage this situation, and it puts the Prison Service and the courts

in a difficult position because, obviously, if somebody is self-declaring that they have to be recognised, then they have to be dealt with on that basis, even though physically, they have not have [*sic*] made the transformation.[31]

The Scottish government overlooked both the objections of the public and the evidence from Ireland, but it could not ignore the UK government. Scotland is not a sovereign state: it is a constituent part of the United Kingdom. Shortly after Christmas, the secretary of state for Scotland – a UK government minister – did indeed react to concerns over the impact on the Equality Act and blocked the Scottish Gender Recognition Reform Bill from becoming law. If there was a constitutional crisis, it became a personal crisis for Nicola Sturgeon. Her scope for manoeuvre became limited when – in quick succession – two male sex offenders were found to be heading for women's prisons.

Bryson the rapist was one; the other went by the name of 'Tiffany Scott'. Scott was a violent offender serving an indefinite sentence after admitting stalking a thirteen-year-old girl by sending letters from prison. Scott will only be released when no longer considered to be an 'unmanageable risk to public safety'.[32] It did not matter that neither Bryson nor Scott had a GRC, because the Scottish Prison Service was already 'ahead of the law'. Indeed, local transgender activists had worked on prison policy specifically. In 2018, the director of the Scottish Trans Alliance wrote: 'We strategized that by working intensively with the Scottish Prison Service to support them to include trans women as women on a self-declaration basis within very challenging circumstances, we would be able to ensure that all other public services should be able to do likewise.'[33]

Those tactics might have worked while the public was unaware of them, but the outcome was now front-page news. But whatever law or policy might dictate, we all know the difference between men and women: it is instinctive. Any politician trying to defend laws that require a male rapist to be treated as a woman is in for a difficult time. No wonder that the Dentons document advised activists to 'avoid excessive press coverage and exposure'.

For Nicola Sturgeon, there were awkward questions at every interview. Seemingly unable to declare that Isla Bryson – a fully intact male rapist, remember – was a woman for fear of what an incredulous public might think, and unwilling to torpedo her own self-ID legislation by declaring Bryson to be a man, she prevaricated. Within weeks, amidst a cluster of political storms, she resigned as first minister.

But, elsewhere in the world, self-ID bills continued to become law, and sometimes against steep resistance. Speak Up for Women New Zealand campaigned strongly against the part of the Births, Deaths, Marriages, and Relationships Registration Bill that introduced self-ID in that country.[34] The bill had started out as a simple measure to 'develop new digital and online channels to access births, deaths and marriages information'. Those profound changes – to allow anyone to change their legal sex for whatever reason they might have – were slipped in after the initial public consultation had closed.

In Spain, the organisation Contra el Borrado de las Mujeres (Against the Erasure of Women) fought against *la Ley Trans* ('the Trans Law'), passed in February 2023. In their words: 'The substitution of the sex category for that of gender identity turns the definition of woman into something completely subjective and that affects our material reality in many different areas.'[35] They cited sport, education, statistics, legislation, health and safe spaces, as well as pointing out the attack on language and the impact on children and lesbian women.

But while both New Zealand and Spain enshrined self-ID in law, the UK has not. The juggernaut that was unleashed in Yogyakarta has not yet overrun Great Britain, or 'TERF Island', as it has been dubbed.[36] It is the place where I live as a transsexual.

Other trans people have apparently been trying to flee. One was reported to have said: 'I'm upset at seeing what the UK has become. They want to erase trans people. That is the only end goal. It is so dangerous, and anyone who thinks that this will stop at trans people is delusional.' Other countries are seen to be far safer than England's 'casual transphobia and a constant feeling of dread'. Another trans person, who was trying to relocate to Germany, was quoted as saying: 'It's so nice here. It's much easier to be queer in Germany. You see people being openly affectionate in the supermarkets here. In England, you're always looking over your shoulder, worried about how other people will react.'[37]

Individual anecdotes can of course be found to support whatever claim anyone wishes to assert. But it is ludicrous to suggest that the UK has become a place where it is difficult for trans people to survive, let alone prosper. It's not true – certainly in my experience. I go about my daily life much as I have always done since I transitioned. I continue to work as a teacher, and I still support my colleagues as their union rep. Outside school, I am involved in a range of social activities. The truth is that people could hardly care less that I am trans – if they notice, that is.

I have experienced very little outright transphobia in real life. Even when it has occurred, it has never involved middle-aged women campaigning for their sex-based rights. The usual culprits are groups of young men, perhaps fuelled by alcohol. However, it's probably not just trans people who would be advised to give those groups a wide berth. But I have come across curiosity. One elderly woman approached me at a Tube station in central London. It was well into the evening, so the platform was quiet. Her question was direct and to the point: 'Are you one of them blokes?'

What to do with that, I thought. Certainly, it was clear that I was in no danger. She was much smaller than me and she was laden with groceries. I tried the direct response: 'Why yes, so I am!'

She looked up at me for a moment, before adding: 'You're very convincing.'

'Clearly not convincing enough,' I replied with a smile.

'Good on yer,' came her response. She smiled, nodded and went on her way. The crisis was over. Should I have reported it? I could have done, and perhaps the police would have called her in to be interviewed. Maybe the incident would have been recorded and added to the statistics – perpetuating a false impression of a nation bristling with transphobic hatred.

That was curiosity; on other occasions there might be disagreement, perhaps even criticism of our views, or our way of life. But not hate, and it helps nobody to conflate these things, least of all trans people – some of whom seem fearful about even leaving the house for fear of how others might react to them.

However, while the UK government held firm, pressures were brought on 'TERF Island' from over the channel. The UK might have left the European Union, but we retain our membership of the Council of Europe. Those two organisations are easily confused, and no wonder. The similarly named European Council *is* an EU institution, while both the European Parliament (part of the EU) and the Parliamentary Assembly of the Council of Europe (PACE) meet in Strasbourg.

The Council of Europe is the older and larger of the two organisations. Founded in 1949, it comprises almost all the countries with territory in Europe. Before the Russian Federation was expelled in March 2022, only Belarus, Kazakhstan, Kosovo and the Vatican City were not members.[38] The focus of its work is democracy, the rule of law and human rights. The European Convention on Human Rights (ECHR) is 'the cornerstone of all its activities', while the European Court of Human Rights (ECtHR) was established by the Council of Europe in 1959; it rules on individual or state applications alleging violations of the civil and political rights set out in the ECHR.[39]

Unlike Members of the European Parliament (MEPs), members of PACE are not directly elected. National parliaments elect delegates (and nominated substitutes) to go to Strasbourg for plenary debates held four times a year. PACE has been fertile ground for gender identity ideology. It was the place that in 2015 passed Resolution 2048, which called on member states to introduce self-ID, and cemented in policy the concept of the transgender child.[40]

In 2021, Fourat Ben Chikha, a Green politician from Belgium, authored a PACE report on what he perceived to be 'the extensive and often virulent attacks on the rights of LGBTI people that have been occurring for several years'.[41] His eighteen-page missive, 'Combating rising hate against LGBTI people in Europe', identified five countries: Hungary, Poland, the Russian Federation, Turkey and the United Kingdom. It seemed an unlikely combination. UK society is rather different from the countries he cited in Eastern Europe. But the draft resolution embedded in the report made clear his reasoning. Paragraph 5 stated:

> The Assembly condemns the highly prejudicial anti-gender, gender-critical and anti-trans narratives which reduce the fight for the equality of LGBTI people to what these movements deliberately mis-characterise as 'gender ideology' or 'LGBTI ideology'. Such narratives deny the very existence of LGBTI people, dehumanise them, and often falsely portray their rights as being in conflict with women's and children's rights, or societal and family values in general. All of these are deeply

damaging to LGBTI people, while also harming women's and children's rights and social cohesion.

There *is* an ideology – a system of ideas and ideals – but Ben Chikha clearly wanted PACE to deny it. His explanatory memorandum that followed was even more damning of the UK. The emphasis is mine.

> In the United Kingdom, *anti-trans rhetoric, arguing that sex is immutable* and gender identities not valid, has also been gaining baseless and concerning credibility, at the expense of both trans people's civil liberties and women's and children's rights. At the IDAHOT [International Day against Homophobia, Biphobia and Transphobia] Forum 2021, the Minister for Equalities stated, in contradiction with international human rights standards with respect to the rights of trans people, 'We do not believe in self-identification'…
>
> The 'gender-critical' movement, which wrongly portrays trans rights as posing a particular threat to cisgender women and girls, has played a significant role in this process, notably since the 2018 public consultation on updating the Gender Recognition Act 2004 for England and Wales. In parallel, trans rights organisations have faced vitriolic media campaigns, in which *trans women especially are vilified and misrepresented.*

It's simply nonsense. As far as human beings are concerned, sex *is* immutable. That is a biological fact. Unlike Ben Chikha,

I am a transwoman and I live in the UK. I just don't recognise the vilification that he imagines. But as well as conflating the UK with four very different countries, he also interpreted critical thinking as hate.

As noted above, PACE delegates are not directly elected to Strasbourg, but Ben Chikha was not even directly elected in Belgium. He was a member of the Belgian Senate, whose sixty members are either appointed by regional and community parliaments or co-opted; Ben Chikha was co-opted.[42] But despite the dubious democratic accountability of the author, his report was tabled for debate at the plenary session in January 2022.

Council of Europe resolutions might not be binding on member states, but they carry a lot of weight. In December 2016, Maria Miller cited Council of Europe Resolution 2048 in that Westminster debate following the original Women and Equalities Committee report on transgender equality. It's hard for anyone to counter such evidence unless they are sure of themselves and certain of the facts.

This time, however, some members of the UK delegation had prepared carefully. They tabled ten amendments in a valiant attempt to rescue the resolution. Just three managed to find their way into the final text. Crucially, the word 'sex' was inserted into paragraph 12.1:

> amend criminal legislation as necessary to ensure that its provisions with respect to hate crimes clearly cover all offences committed against a person or group of persons based on their sex, sexual orientation, gender identity, gender expression and sex characteristics,

include proportionate and dissuasive sanctions, protect victims' rights and make provision for them to receive compensation.[43]

An attempt to extract the UK from the naughty step failed despite a powerful yet conciliatory speech from Labour MP Tonia Antoniazzi.[44] She did not merely object to the UK's inclusion alongside Hungary, Poland, Russia and Turkey, she drilled down into the data that Ben Chikha had cited in his report. That included the 2021 annual review by ILGA Europe, an NGO which advocates for the 'human rights and equality for LGBTI people at European level'.[45] ILGA's evidence painted a rather different picture, as Antoniazzi explained to the chamber: 'The [ILGA] Review links the data source, Rainbow Europe. In the rank order of forty-nine European countries, the UK was placed fifth in respect of hate crime and hate speech. I want to underline that, it was fifth.'

Not the fifth worst, but the fifth best. This is the truth that the proponents of gender identity ideology do not like to countenance. It was even a battle to put the amendment to a vote. Antoniazzi needed the support of at least ten colleagues. But under COVID regulations, this was a hybrid session and, in a display of anti-democratic farce, those logging in remotely were unable to register their support.

This led to a dramatic intervention by Lord Foulkes – a Labour member of the House of Lords – who interrupted the debate to express his frustration: 'We raised points of order and we were ignored.'[46] After he was supported by an unlikely alliance of Jeremy Corbyn from the left and Lord

Howell from the right, a vote was eventually taken.[47] But nevertheless, Antoniazzi's amendment to remove the words 'and the United Kingdom' fell by 61 votes to 23.

When the resolution itself – Council of Europe Resolution 2417 – was carried 72 to 12, the UK found itself condemned, on paper at least, for something it had not done. I live here and I recognise the evidence Antoniazzi cited in her speech: the UK is one of the best countries in Europe in terms of hate crime and hate speech.

Following on from Antoniazzi in debate, the Conservative Lord Blencathra put his finger on what the motion was really getting at. In his speech he said, quite succinctly: 'What it appears to be suggesting is that UK society suffers from bigotry by allowing an open discussion about introducing new laws about self-identification of gender.'[48]

At least the debate was recorded for posterity, so that it can be rekindled should anyone try to use Council of Europe Resolution 2417 in the way that Maria Miller cited number 2048. Much has changed in the UK since that Westminster debate in 2016, and in my mind for the better – certainly, for women and children. At the same time a light has been shone on transgender rights. But those rights were never secure when they were based on feelings. Here on TERF Island, reality is dawning. Gender identity ideology is no longer lapped up without analysis or critical thought. Trans people can be protected against harassment and discrimination – and hate speech – without imposing the pretence that we are somehow the same as the other sex. And, crucially, impinging on the rights of women.

9

CHILDREN AND TECHNOLOGY

I HAVE worked with children for nearly thirty years. Much has changed – when I qualified as a teacher in 1996, there was no computer on my desk and the word 'projector' referred to the OHP that trundled into my classroom on a trolley. Email was a novelty – that we checked sporadically – phones plugged into the wall, and internal messages were still hand-written on memos and left in pigeonholes. Modern social media had yet to reach me, or the children I taught.

The impact of gender identity ideology on children has been significant and – I would argue – deleterious. But it's inconceivable that such a bizarre concept could have taken root without social media to nurture it. The rise of social media is surely comparable to the invention of the printing press. But while Gutenberg's innovation facilitated the easy dissemination of information, social media allows virtually anyone to publish whatever they like, and be heard by anyone who is prepared to listen. As a result, new communities have sprung up whose members are divorced completely from their physical bodies. We might still be encapsulated in a few dozen kilos of carbon, hydrogen, oxygen and various other elements arranged into a complex life form, but our minds and our ideas have been let loose in cyberspace.

On social media platforms we can recreate ourselves as we would like to be seen. Images can be filtered and enhanced, or replaced by avatars, while names – or handles? – can be changed on a whim. We can maintain multiple identities at the same time; we are limited only by time and energy, and possibly the need to make a living. This separation of mind and body is profound, and it has happened in less than one generation. We were social beings in 1996, and so we remain. But we cannot expect those evolved instincts that protect us in the physical world to transfer seamlessly to those new communities in the virtual universe where bodies are absent.

Sex, that fundamental pillar of human society, takes on new meaning online. In the material world, sex is binary and immutable. But not so in cyberspace. Divorced from our potential role in reproduction, 'gender' can be changed as easily as we can change a handle and an avatar. And why stop at two? Perhaps it's not surprising that the non-binary phenomenon among young people followed the rise of social media.

But while we might leave our bodies behind, we cannot so easily ignore our instincts. My experience playing internet chess proves that point nicely. Away from the gender debate I am just another anonymous Debbie. I don't declare my sex – why should it matter? Chess is a game we play with our minds rather than our bodies. But I do use my own photograph as an avatar. I know that my opponents assume that I am female because of the messages they leave in the chat box. 'Hello gorgeous, you look stunning today' is an opening gambit that does not involve the loss of a pawn.

This is irrational behaviour: anyone could be lurking behind my profile. But it is hard to shake off our instincts even when we are conscious of them. Evolution did not prepare us for the internet. When we see a photograph of a woman we assume we are messaging a woman, and instinct takes over. Few players attempt to chat me up, but the sexual dynamic might still explain why I am never short of matches to play. At the time of writing, I have eighteen simultaneous games underway, but I am playing black in seventeen of them. The reason is in the structure of the app – a male competitor opens up the game with white, and I respond. When games swing my way, more than once I have been asked, 'Is your boyfriend playing your moves for you, love?'

Online it was easy for me to become a woman in their minds – all it took was a name and a photograph. But sex perception – a skill vital for our survival – evolved to be used in real life. We know that there are two sexes and that there are only two sexes. We read the signals, and we make up our minds. It is an instinct ingrained in our psychology and it cannot be easily ignored.

Schröder's stairs, an optical illusion first published in 1858, is also a binary where we read the signals and make a decision. Our brains interpret this two-dimensional diagram as a three-dimensional staircase. We can easily imagine a cartoon figure walking up the stairs from right to left.

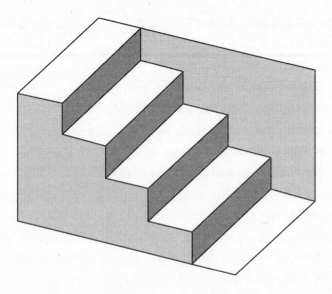

Schröder's Stairs: An optical illusion named after Heinrich G. F. Schröder, who published it in 1858

Turn the page upside down, however, and something remarkable happens. We know that the image has been rotated so – initially at least – we might see a staircase viewed from below. But the moment we blink, our brains reinterpret the image into that more familiar perspective on the world and – once again – we find ourselves looking down on the stairs from above. No matter how hard our conscious minds try to frustrate our instincts, we evolved to survive in a world where we did not have the luxury of thinking about every signal that enters our minds.

So it is with sex. In real life we read the signals whenever we meet someone new, whatever their pronoun badge might say. Young people who have grown up with the internet risk perpetual disappointment if they expect their online cross-sex or non-binary identity to translate effortlessly into the real world, where bodies speak for themselves.

But while this out-of-body method of interacting is a new phenomenon, there are parallels in history. Two millennia before the internet, Gnosticism became an early heresy in the Christian Church. In the early second century, Gnostics separated the spiritual from the material. They held that matter was evil and the spirit good. Their focus was on the person of Jesus Christ – claims were made that he did not have a real body but only an apparent or phantom one – and a hope of salvation that came through esoteric knowledge, or gnosis.

Gnosticism was first refuted by Ignatius of Antioch, who died around 110 CE, but the desire to escape our mortal being never went away.[1] Adherents of gender identity ideology may replace spirit with mind, but the schism between mind and body is much the same. Like those early Gnostics, their entire belief system is constructed on mysterious knowledge.

But just because we want something does not mean that we can have it. Those desires may be impossible to satisfy – we are still human, after all. Human beings are body as well as mind, but that has not stopped idealists trying to break the link. Unlike transsexualism, which changed the body to make it congruent with the mind – or so the theory goes – the recent non-binary phenomenon goes further. At least there are female and male bodies for transsexuals to emulate, but, in real life, nobody has a non-binary body: we all have a sexed body, and it is male or female.

Despite the attempts of LGBTQIA+ activists to claim that the 'T' proves we can be between male and female, everybody – intersex people included – belongs to a species that has just two sexes, male and female. After all, each one of us has exactly two biological parents – one of each sex – just like every other sexually dimorphic species this Earth has accommodated now and in the past. But that absolute binary does not apply to our minds, at least not in the same way. Male and female psychologies do tend to follow different patterns, most obviously in the context of sexual attraction. Most men are sexually attracted to women, and most women are sexually attracted to men.

Anyone familiar with the Myers–Briggs Type Indicator will be aware of the two decision-making functions: thinking and feeling.[2] In this context, thinking prioritises objective principles and impersonal facts, while feeling elevates personal concerns and the people involved. Everyone uses both functions – perhaps in different proportions at different times – but many people have a preference for one or the other. Studies show that most men are thinking-preference while women have a tendency to be feeling-preference.[3] That bias is hardly unexpected, but it can be politically awkward in modern Western societies, as summarised by the authors of one academic paper: 'Some argue that even if they are small, actual, verifiable (not artefactual) sex differences, they should not be explored or explained because of the divisive personal and social effect that it can have on both sexes.'[4]

But these differences are between the two populations as a whole. They do not necessarily constrain individuals within each group. Variety is the spice of life. Same-sex attraction certainly exists, while I am married to a thinking-preference woman. There might be two different patterns of human psychologies, but each person has some degree of all personality traits. They lie on a spectrum within each sex, and these can overlap.

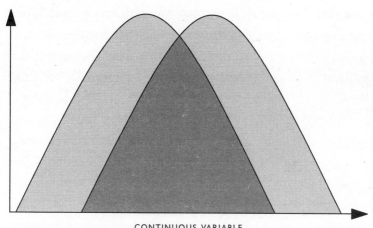

Two overlapping distributions. The variable plotted on the horizontal axis is continuous, indicating patterns of variation in each group that can overlap.

However the data falls, there are still two sexes. While this line graph might show measurements related to personality traits overlapping, they are also the traits of people who can be categorised male and female, shown as a bar chart. Even rare intersex conditions occur within one sex or the other – not outside them, nor between them.

Both diagrams describe human beings, but in different ways. My subject, physics, is noted for the phenomenon of wave–particle duality: electrons can be described as waves or particles. They travel from one place to another like waves but, when they get to their destination, they interact with the target like particles. Human beings can perhaps be attributed a psychological–physiological duality: mind and body. Both are valid, and both are necessary. We think with our minds, and then we communicate with our bodies – or we did. But then came the smartphone.

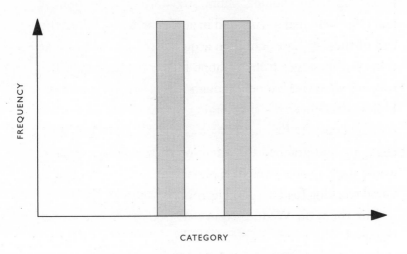

Two separate categories: the variable plotted on the horizontal axis is categoric, indicating two separate groups that are distinct from each other.

By 2011, half the UK population owned one.[5] Then, according to Ofcom, 2015 was the first year in which 'the smartphone was considered to be the most important device for accessing the internet among all adults, overtaking the laptop'.[6] The internet now followed us around in our pocket. We could stay connected to the internet continuously if we wished, perhaps even take up residence there, only visiting the real world to eat and drink, and for other essential bodily functions. In a world that had no need for bodies, those non-binary identities proliferated. Youngsters have known nothing else.

Some places, however, remained strictly real-world. Many schools had strong policies on mobile phone usage. As a teacher I was instructed to be vigilant. Children were not to use them and, should a phone stray into my classroom, it had to be switched off, handed in and not returned until the end of the day. Later, children acquired smart watches that conveyed messages from a phone hidden in their bag. The watches were also banned, though maybe with less success. Holding the line against emerging technology was another task to fill my day. But one thing was sure. When lessons were engaging and grabbed the attention of the class, messages would stack up unanswered on phones in the bottoms of bags. Good teaching fostered good learning better than any policy.

But then, on Wednesday, 18 March 2020, the world changed. The prime minister told us that, within forty-eight hours, schools would close to most pupils 'until further notice'.[7] The World Health Organization had recently declared COVID-19 to be a pandemic, and there were fears for public health.[8] By the time Boris Johnson made his announcement, it already felt inevitable. But while the news was not surprising, it was still shocking. Schools had not been closed during wartime; now they were closing indefinitely. We had two days in school to put Operation Remote Teaching into action. I had never used the preferred video conferencing software before – nor had many of my colleagues – but the following Monday we taught lessons from our homes by webcam. Teachers are often at our best in a crisis, and we made it work as best we could.

Online lessons were a new experience for everybody, but, as the novelty wore off, the level of engagement from my pupils was mixed. School – possibly their most significant real-world experience – was reduced to an app on their phone. The temptation to stray into social media was right there in their hands. During live lessons they could see me but, due to hastily instigated safeguarding policies, all I could see on my monitor was an array of black rectangles labelled with a name or an avatar. Some children followed my lessons more closely than others. When it was time to go some of those rectangles lingered and did not respond to enquiries – likely the children had disappeared long before. There was little I could do apart from inform senior colleagues, who could do little more.

That situation persisted for the rest of that school year and for most of the spring term the following year. For two terms, children were kept out of the real world. The impact on them and their developing minds should not be underestimated. For those who struggled with their sexed bodies, the temptation to retreat from reality must have been overwhelming. Online, they could change their 'gender' as easily as their handle or avatar and experience life in the other 'gender' – possibly without parents, and certainly not distant teachers, having any clue who those children were communicating with, and what messages they were absorbing.

These youngsters' experience bears little resemblance to my memories of 2012, the year I transitioned. Bodies mattered, and many of us – me included – clung to the idea that we had been born in the wrong body. We transitioned in the real world but well away from the news agenda. We identified what we thought was the problem, then went to our family doctors for a referral to a Gender Identity Clinic. Transsexualism was a curious medical issue that involved a tiny number of people. And the vast majority of us were adults.

Today, 'Trans lives matter' is shouted across the internet. Of course they matter – we are human beings, after all. But we have also seemingly been elevated into a priestly class. Another social media slogan, 'Trans bodies are sacred', proves my claim nicely. But what does that actually mean? Aren't all bodies equally sacred (or not), according to your religious persuasion? But this is a new way of thinking that shares the language of, and blurs the boundary with, religion. In 2022 a group of senior figures from several Christian denominations, including Rowan Williams, former Archbishop of Canterbury, lobbied the prime minister to ban so-called conversion therapy. In their letter, they suggested that 'to be trans is to enter a sacred journey of becoming whole: precious, honoured and loved, by yourself, by others and by God'.[9] It was a truly astonishing claim. In response, another prominent Christian wrote:

In one sentence this brings into the open what a good deal of the LGBT+ movement has become: it is now a sacred quest, an agenda no longer driven by science, common sense, or simple compassion; but by a transcendental vision, a desire for mystical fulfilment and a metaphysical belief in unseen realities. This is, more than anything else, a religion.[10]

The writer went on to call it 'a religion of enlightenment by bodily modification'. That is true, but equally it is a religion of bodily denial. Trans people are that priestly class because we have led the way. When we hear that 'transwomen are women, transmen are men and non-binary identities are valid', we might be listening to the veneration of people who are seen to have transcended the physical world and escaped their mortal shells. If we are that priestly class, then it follows that we are also good people. In the second century, Ignatius of Antioch might have dismissed Gnosticism as heresy, but today impressionable children lap up gender identity ideology as the answer to all their problems.

The truth is mundane. My body is no more sacred than anyone else's, and gender identity disorders are just that – disorders. Maybe in Ignatius's day psychological disorders would have been explained away as demons? But whatever is happening, it is part of the human condition. We did not need to invent a new belief system to explain it away, and we certainly did not need to sell it to children.

Tragically, some children have been subjected to life-changing physical interventions. Puberty blockers may have stopped their natural development so that they will never know what it means to grow up the way nature intended.

Studies have shown that almost all of that group are on a conveyor belt to cross-sex hormones, the long-term effects of which are unknown.[11] This is truly experimental treatment. Some teenage girls will never be able to breastfeed their own babies after electing to have a double mastectomy. The LGBT+ community might call it 'top surgery', but the procedure is the same. One plastic surgeon – Dr Sidhbh Gallagher – has touted her business on social media, where she styles herself 'Dr Teetus Deletus'.[12] Her videos are glitzy and her language is juvenile, but her product is profound and permanent.

Of course, not every child who struggles with their sex will undergo such catastrophic – and irreversible – surgery, but the impact of gender identity ideology is felt widely in schools. After nearly thirty years in the classroom, I know that some children struggle with their changing bodies. Others struggle to cope with the changing nature of relationships among their peer group, both within their sex and between the sexes. Growing up is hard – it always has been. But what is new is the concept of the 'trans' person, and by extension, the so-called 'trans child'.

According to gender identity ideology, the trans child is a young person who does not identify with the gender that was assigned to them at birth. It must sound tantalising to children who struggle with their sex. The message has been proselytised with the help of 'genderbread persons' and 'gender unicorns': bright, cheerfully coloured cartoon images that push the concept of gender identity onto children, who believe what they are told.[13]

The creators of the unicorn defined gender identity as

> one's internal sense of being male, female, neither of
> these, both, or another gender(s). Everyone has a gender
> identity, including you. For transgender people, their sex
> assigned at birth and their own internal sense of gender
> identity are not the same. Female, woman, and girl and
> male, man, and boy are also not necessarily linked to each
> other but are just six common gender identities.[14]

This is simply not true. Those concepts *are* linked, and we are male or female in the same way that each member of every other mammalian species is male or female. Females produce large gametes – called ova, or eggs – while males produce small motile gametes called sperm. Sperm meets egg and the cycle starts all over again. Adult female humans are called 'women' and adult male humans are called 'men'; juveniles are called 'girls' and 'boys' respectively. There is certainly variation within each sex, but that variation accounts for everyone.

We all used to know this, and we accepted it even if we didn't like it. But now children have been told that the traditional view of sex is somewhat simplistic (it isn't), that scientists have found out more (which they might have done, but there are still two immutable sexes), and that not everyone falls into the binary (they do). When these ideas come into schools, they can go virtually unchallenged.

As COVID restrictions were relaxed, schools reverted to more typical forms of education. Back in the classroom, children were again a captive audience. But some teachers had embraced gender identity ideology and promoted it with sincerity and enthusiasm. Perhaps they genuinely believed that it would improve their pupils' lives? Other teachers might shrug and pay lip service. After all, if it makes some people feel happier about themselves, it can't be a bad thing, can it? Actually – behind the rainbows and sparkles – it can be very bad.

Few secondary-school teachers train to be teachers of PSHE – personal, social, health and economic education; rather, we are physics teachers, or teachers of maths, English, geography, art, whatever. Most primary-school teachers *are* expected to be able to teach across the curriculum, but few are PSHE specialists. For many teachers, the PSHE programme is something that needs to be covered, perhaps with their tutor group after taking the register and reading out the notices for the day. 'Just give us a scheme and we will deliver it' is a typical approach.

Schemes of work, and the lesson plans to deliver them, take time and effort to develop – resources that many teachers simply do not have. Understandably, schools have bought ready-to-teach materials from external providers. These are not hard to find. Stonewall UK, for example, claims to have a 'dedicated team of education professionals' who work hard to 'bring you the resources and guidance you need regardless of whether you're just getting started with your LGBTQ+ inclusive work or whether you're looking to further embed and develop your practice'.[15]

Teachers struggling to find the time to mark their books suddenly have one less job to worry about. As Stonewall says:

'Whether you're looking for best practice guidance and policy templates, posters or lesson packs written by a qualified teacher, there's something here for you.' Job done! But what job has been done, and why has it been done?

Gender identity ideology can indeed look harmless at first glance. But behind the bright and colourful resources – including the genderbread persons and gender unicorns – adults are making promises that they can never deliver. Youngsters are taught that they can choose to identify as boys, girls or perhaps something else. Children have always harboured fantasies; our job as teachers should not be to affirm them uncritically, but gently and sensitively to steer them back to reality. Of course, we should protect gender non-conforming children from condemnation, criticism and ridicule, but we need not cite gender identity. Crucially, nobody should need to claim to be trans or non-binary in order to be respected for being different.

Opting out from gender identity ideology is hard. The Karpman drama triangle comprises three positions: persecutor, victim and rescuer.[16] When conflicts occur, good people (rescuers) might help other good people (victims) keep safe from bad people (persecutors). When transgender-identified children are framed as victims, the message to adults is binary – are you a rescuer or a persecutor? Those who question gender identity ideology risk being labelled as persecutors, and shamed until they comply.

Gender identity ideology, however, not only needs to be questioned – it must be challenged. It is not harmless: it imposes unscientific and – I would argue – harmful ideas on children. Youngsters need to grow up and find themselves, not be railroaded into off-the-peg identities. The BBC was criticised for its 'over 100 genders' claim, but in some respects it didn't go far enough. Every human being is unique: if there are 7 billion of us then there are also 7 billion different genders.

But for all the variation in personality, there are just two sexes. Science cannot be fooled even if people can be. Boys who yearn to express femininity do not need to become girls as part of the deal. Meanwhile, girls who are desperate to eschew that same femininity don't need to identify as non-binary to cut their hair, wear trousers and climb trees. Nobody needs a gender identity – we simply need to be ourselves.

Grasping that point is hard; articulating it is harder. Gender identity ideology might be new, but the pressure to conform to the group is not. In my childhood, we picked football teams to support, or perhaps bands to follow. Cultures grew up around those choices, and they were sometimes intense. Looking back, those decisions were not made freely. But we didn't need others to direct us – we did it to ourselves. FOMO, the fear of missing out – perhaps another evolved instinct – was enough. I might have been headstrong, even then, but I conformed with my peers. In the north-east of England in the 1980s, that meant Newcastle United and heavy metal. I still follow the former and listen to the latter – I am the result of my childhood – but my choices were activities, not identities: they might interest me, even entertain me, but they do not define me.

Gender identities, on the other hand, have a profound effect. Social pressures that today's children experience not only have an impact on what they do, they change who they are – even the names they call themselves and the pronouns they declare. Not only that, gender identity ideology supports a ready-made community in which transgender-identified children are applauded into the priestly class.

If, in 1980, a teacher had told me that I could be a girl, I would have been all ears. If they had told me that there were drugs and surgeries that could make me look like a girl, my next question would have been 'Where do I find them?' That was the stuff of my dreams. Throw in an affirming community and I would have been desperate to sign up for the full package. It would have been a mistake – transition is not an elixir – but I do not think I would have discerned that truth as a child. Years later, when the opportunity did arise, the compulsion to transition overwhelmed me. By that time, I was a mature adult in my forties, but even then it took half a decade before I recognised that the availability of the treatment had driven my need for it. In effect, I realised that I had been an addict.

Had someone told me that the treatment was available to others, but not to me, I would have been mentally crushed. 'Peak FOMO' does not start to do justice to the intensity of the emotions that other people's transition videos generated in me until I went through with a transition of my own. It is much easier to live with unachievable dreams – as I did throughout childhood – than it is to cope with the realisation that the magic treatment is just out of reach.

I feel for today's transgender-identified children and I worry greatly about them, but I do not get involved. My job is to teach physics, not to counsel children in psychological distress. Twice since I transitioned, pupils have approached me with issues of their own around sex and gender. On both occasions I followed the normal school policy on disclosures. I advised them that I might need to share their news with trusted colleagues. Then I listened, after which I conferred with colleagues on the pastoral-support team. In both cases, that was my only role in the matter. One child transitioned soon after leaving school, while the other experimented with a non-binary identity. I hope they received the professional help and support that they needed, but that was not my business. I might be transsexual, but life experience is no substitute for expertise: transgender-identified children are not helped by well-meaning teachers – trans or otherwise – doing what they think is best.

Senior teachers sometimes ask me to advise on trans policies. I'm not a policy expert, but two general principles seem to me to be self-evident. Firstly, we cannot change our sex and nor can we wish it away. In schools, we sometimes need to treat boys and girls differently – in sports, changing rooms and toilets, for example. In these situations, biological sex matters and transgender-identified children must not be accommodated with the other sex.

The second principle is inclusion. That does not mean placing boys in girls' spaces, or vice versa, but they can and should be included in mixed-sex spaces with everyone else. Schools should also be sympathetic to pupils who prefer to opt out of stereotypes bundled with their sex. Boys and girls do not need separate uniform codes, for example. That doesn't mean putting every child in nondescript trousers and sweatshirts, but it does mean allowing girls to wear trousers. A boy may need rather more courage to wear a skirt, but his sex should not stop him.

Most British names tend to refer to just one sex, but that is simply convention, usage or tradition. Some names are used by both sexes. Ashley, for example, is my own middle name, and I saw no need to change it when I transitioned. Leslie and Leigh have switched between the sexes. Preferred names can be used in place of our legal names and we can change them for a host of different reasons.

The crucial point is that no child should need to identify as the opposite sex before they are allowed to wear clothes in which they feel comfortable, or use their preferred name – George was a girl in Enid Blyton's Famous Five – or perhaps study their preferred subjects. Gender non-conformity can be tolerated – celebrated even – without the need to pretend that any child is really the opposite sex, or has a gender identity. But schools and teachers have been seduced to the point where they no longer recognise reality. I've seen that myself.

The whole school stopped for house cross country. It was a key annual event; lessons were cancelled so that every child could take part and make their way round the circuit. Boys and girls ran alongside each other. At the finishing line, they were all assigned a number in the order they finished. With no physics to teach that afternoon I was assigned to the recording desk. My job was to record numbers on two enormous lists of names. Boys were on one side, and girls on the other, so that we could disaggregate the data to produce a rank order for each sex in each age group. Simple!

But how should we record the finishing times of pupils who identified as non-binary? A colleague came to me in a state of apology. It had been decided, I was told, that they would be included with their birth sex, so I would need to look for their names on that list. Was I OK with that? And please could I be sensitive when non-binary pupils arrived at the recording desk.

I reassured my colleague that I had no problems with the instruction. Never in the past had we grouped runners according to how they felt about themselves, and we didn't need to start now. But gender identity ideology had obfuscated something that really did matter in sport – biological sex. When those children finished, I took their numbers, and I wrote them alongside their names in the same way that I recorded every other child. There was no fuss and I made no reference to their sex. There was just no need: we can be kind without telling lies. I have many concerns for children who identify as trans or non-binary, but getting them off social media and running in the fresh air is a step in the right direction.

And what is the outlook for transsexual adults – me, for example? There I also have concerns. For years we existed under the radar. When we were noticed we might have generated a degree of prurient interest. But so long as we fitted into the society around us – albeit making a concerted effort to be perceived as the other sex – we were allowed to get on with our lives. But the events of the past ten years have put us under the spotlight, and much is different. The future is now uncertain, and past performance is no guarantee of future results.

10

THE TRANSSEXUAL FUTURE

IN little more than ten years, the world in which we trans-sexuals live our lives has changed beyond all recognition. In 2012 I transitioned as a means to an end – to protect my sanity. Like other transsexuals, my objective was to restore my mental health and reassimilate into society, living *as a member of the other sex*. What that meant in practice, of course, was being per-ceived to be a member of the other sex. Hard work, hormone therapy and surgery could create an illusion strong enough to tip the balance in the minds of others. Within transsexual support groups we called that 'passing'. Transsexuals who were routinely read as the opposite sex had no need for pronoun badges. We were known to exist, but few people expected to come across us; if we were perceived to be the opposite sex then we were assumed to be the opposite sex. Indeed, for transsex-uals, coming out was far less important than staying hidden.

Little more than a decade later, even the word 'transsex-ual' has been displaced. We have been subsumed under the 'transgender' umbrella, and the former term can be frowned upon. Stonewall suggests that it was 'used in the past… many people prefer the term trans or transgender'.[1] Others go further in their disdain for the label. In the United States, the organisation PFLAG – formerly the Parents and Friends of Lesbians and Gays – indicates that the word 'transsexual' is 'considered by some to be outdated or possibly offensive'.[2]

Change has not been limited to the language we are urged to use. Social attitudes have moved on, and not necessarily for the better. While support is surely preferable to indifference, some of those enthusiastic trans allies – corporations as well as individuals – are a mixed blessing. Sometimes I wonder who they think they are helping. Their campaigns hardly align with my goals in life. Like other transsexuals, my objective was to be accepted as a human being and treated no less favourably than other human beings. Given the choice, I would always prefer to be affirmed as a parent, a teacher or perhaps a writer, than to be labelled as transgender. Or – even worse – victimised so that others can rescue me. Yes, I have battled with an unusual psychological condition, but transsexualism does not define me any more than my short-sightedness does.

Gender reassignment is a far more significant process than buying a pair of spectacles, but they are both disorders that have been treated so that I can live a normal life. Neither process, however, cured the original condition. I'm still short-sighted – and struggle to find my glasses when I have taken them off – and I am still attracted to the thought of myself as a woman. But while it might not have been a cure, gender reassignment was a palliative solution that treated the symptoms.

But that is not the way the modern transgender community see things. Their way of thinking sets transgender people apart, and assigns them a gender identity that labels them and – it seems to me – defines them. While transsexualism describes something I *did*, transgender is something they *are*. In terms of language, it was a simple verb swap: *to do* was replaced by *to be*. But the impact on society was profound. Gender identity ideology permeated our institutions and changed the narrative. Transgender people are now at the centre of a quasi-religious belief system with its own doctrines and creeds. It's self-serving and inward looking – it certainly doesn't look like progress to me.

This new approach reversed the process of acceptance. Previously, everything was grounded in the perception of others. When hard work, hormone therapy and surgery had done their thing, it made sense for authorities to reissue identity documents such as passports and driving licences with sex markers that matched the perception of others rather than the biological sex of the individual. That was especially true if there was widespread discrimination against those whose presentation did not match their biological sex. But it also avoided the need to explain every time an immigration officer asks: 'Are you sure this is your passport, madam?'

Full legal gender recognition – Gender Recognition Certificates and the consequent changes to birth certificates – took that one step further. But changes to paperwork were understood to follow a decision to 'live as the opposite sex' or 'live in the acquired gender'. Those five words, however, are easier to articulate than explain. Do men and women *really* live in different ways? Language frames communication, but it also limits our thoughts. Such a poor choice of words – men and women are *not* distinguished by the way they live – has led to sloppy thinking and badly drafted laws. The requirement to 'live in the acquired gender', for example, is fundamental to the UK Gender Recognition Act.[3]

Had law and policy instead referred to *perception* – and defined a transsexual person as one routinely perceived to be the other sex – then things might have been different. The law could have been applied in exactly the same way as it turned out, on the basis of reports from medical professionals. I never bothered to apply for a GRC, but I was offered hormone therapy following two psychiatric reports, one of which described my presentation as 'straightforwardly feminine in terms of clothing, mannerisms and overall appearance'. If that sentence ticked the box marked 'living as a woman', it would no doubt also satisfy an alternative criterion: 'perceived to be a woman'.

But, crucially, the word 'perception' implies that other people are necessarily involved. It would have been harder to reduce the process to what is in effect an individual's assertion of their own identity. And, in doing so, to sweep away the barriers to entry – hard work, hormones and surgery, perhaps? – and prepare the ground for self-ID to be incorporated into both policy and public discourse.

In this new world, the old rules no longer work. If self-ID means what it says on the tin, then anyone has the right to self-identify as trans, and any man can claim the label 'transwoman'. Indeed, the only people who cannot be transwomen are women. It was always an imposition on women to expect them to accept transwomen into their groups and their spaces, but those old barriers limited the impact. Now they are gone, and they cannot be plausibly restored. As I predicted back in 2016: 'Transwomen in particular may find that goodwill is replaced by suspicion should abusive men spot an opportunity to exploit women's spaces and protections.'[4] Of course they did.

Perhaps even more damaging to the rights of transsexuals was the reframing of trans people as that priestly class – immune from criticism and, at the same time, weak and vulnerable. Political activists found that they could act with impunity when they flew the pink-and-blue transgender flag and styled themselves as trans allies. Anarchists and rabble-rousers could hardly miss the opportunity that was offered to them on a plate. Trans rights ceased to relate to necessary protections against harassment and discrimination. Those rights were already secure. Instead, 'trans rights' became a rallying call for anyone looking to pick a fight.

But much as some might like just to turn back the clock, the weaknesses in law and policy were there from the start. Any process that grants male people the rights of female people is open to abuse. The only difference is that now everybody knows. 'Old-school' transsexuals who pass flawlessly will no doubt be able to keep their heads down and go unnoticed, as indeed they always have done. Reasonably well-passing transsexuals will likely still be treated in the same way as the sex they resemble: human instinct will see to that. However, the days of being given the benefit of the doubt are maybe gone. Even within friendship groups, women's boundaries are weakened by the inclusion of transwomen. As a female friend once said to me: 'We have no problems with you, Debbie, but if we let you in [to single-sex spaces] then it is much harder to keep out those who are a problem.'

However, transsexualism is unlikely to disappear, and we cannot uninvent hormone therapy or gender reassignment surgery. Even if those treatments are banned in the UK, hormones can be sourced from overseas and surgeons would continue to practise elsewhere in the world. In the 1950s, transsexuals travelled to Morocco for surgery; these days, many seek treatment in Thailand. Those people will need to be accommodated somehow when they return home, but that does not mean the opposite sex should be expected to give up their sex-based rights in the process.

Indeed if – as transwomen – we genuinely respect the members of the sex that we claim to identify with, we need to recognise their boundaries. That does not mean that we should use the men's: that would be a false dichotomy. Using male facilities creates a new set of problems. In some situations, we might be at risk of harm, but, more generally, it would simply be awkward. We might still be male but, when human beings interact, perception matters. Males who are routinely perceived to be female will cause discomfort and embarrassment in the men's. Instead, we need to think outside the 'male' and 'female' boxes. Additional single-use facilities can and do work for anyone who does not wish to share communal facilities with their own sex. Modern build-ings tend to include them already. Clear policy is needed and trans people should respect it. Inclusion should not imply the right to access other people's spaces, but the right to be included and treated no less favourably in a society that is – in the UK at least – overwhelmingly mixed-sex.

Greater clarity is also needed in the interpretation of the law. The Equality Act 2010 protects nine separate charac-teristics, including sex and gender reassignment.[5] They are not the same, and blurring the distinction between them has created confusion and damaged confidence. Even the meaning of the word 'sex' is now open to interpretation and legal judgments. Does it mean biological sex, or legal sex – as amended by a Gender Recognition Certificate? In Scotland, Lady Haldane ruled in favour of the latter. Or could it be read as a synonym for gender identity, a sort of 'social' sex? We cannot be sure, because in the English language the meaning of words can change by usage alone.

In 2023, a public campaign by Sex Matters to clarify the Equality Act provoked a parliamentary debate.[6] The campaigners didn't want the word 'biological' to be inserted in the legislation, merely for the law to be made clear.[7] In their view sex should mean what we have always understood it to mean: an immutable characteristic observed at birth. Clarity might restore some confidence, and that can be to everyone's benefit.

Gender reassignment, meanwhile, protects people who have transitioned, or might consider doing so in the future, from discrimination and harassment as a result. Few people would disagree with that principle. But the law does not confer the right to steal rights from others. In 2022, the minister for women and equalities explained that the Equality Act is a 'shield, not a sword' – perhaps that point could be made clearer to the public?[8]

The Gender Recognition Act 2004, on the other hand, *has* been used by one group to inherit the rights of another.[9] Once a Gender Recognition Certificate is issued, it is very difficult for any service provider to prove that a transwoman is not a woman. When every document indicates 'female' and the right to privacy conveyed by the law shrouds the change in secrecy, how can anyone say 'I don't think you are the sex your birth certificate claims that you are'? The GRA might not have been intended as a sword, but it cuts away the ability of women to protect their sex-based rights. It therefore sits uneasily alongside the Equality Act. No wonder that the prospect of self-ID caused such disquiet among women.

The GRA, remember, was introduced to satisfy Articles 8 and 12 of the European Convention on Human Rights.[10] They are, respectively, the right to respect for private and family life and the right to marry. But since the subsequent Marriage (Same Sex Couples) Act 2013, people in the UK can marry someone of either sex. That legislation includes transsexuals with no need for further remedy.[11] Privacy, meanwhile, is a universal right. If measures were introduced to protect everybody's right not to declare their sex, at least in contexts where sex was not an issue, then the GRA might start to look redundant.

Many transsexuals – me included – who never both-ered to apply for a GRC would not mourn the loss of the GRA. For me at least, my relationships with other people matter far more than pieces of paper. If the GRA is to be retained, though, safeguards should be strengthened rather than weakened – for everyone's sake. Those who use a GRC to impose themselves on women also damage the acceptance and credibility of transsexuals. Besides, it is ultimately futile to hide behind government paperwork. We cannot easily ignore our evolved instincts, and we take people as the sex we find them. If a transition is not good enough without a GRC, then it will never be good enough with one.

But where does this leave me, more than a decade after I decided that I was some kind of woman, and eight years since I walked through Charing Cross Hospital to an operating theatre where my body was changed irrevocably?

I no longer think that I am a woman – women are female while I am male – but I have no plans to detransition. For a start, it is impossible to reverse the physical changes to my body. Gender reassignment surgery is a one-way process, and human breasts do not disappear in the absence of oes-trogen. But even if it were possible, I still prefer my body as is it now. Only since GRS have I really been comfortable inside my own skin. It would make no sense to change it to something that I am less happy with. Exogenous testosterone is of course available, but I like the hair on my head, and have no wish for any more of it to grow elsewhere. Instead, I continue to take a low regular dose of oestradiol to protect my bones from osteoporosis.

Maybe I could socially detransition, while maintaining my current hormone dose? On the assumption that my doctor agreed to carry on writing prescriptions, what would that mean in practice? In some contexts – going to the beach, for example – life would be even more complex than it is now. But even when I am fully clothed, I would need to decide between wearing a chest binder and restricting myself to very baggy clothes.

Like most people, I own some clothes that were marketed as unisex, but otherwise I tend to buy them from the women's range. They fit better, and I like them better. I will buy from the men's range when I see something I particularly like, or perhaps when I need something with decent pockets. But so do many women and, in any case, clothes are just clothes. Although I rarely wear make-up and I own little in the way of jewellery, I do like to dress up for special occasions and in a dress rather than a suit.

The length of my hair is more typical of women than men – particularly at my stage in life – but I wear it long because I like it long. If I socially detransitioned, might I need to cut my hair at the same time as throwing out most of my clothes? Or could I simply ignore all the stereotypes, and continue wearing the clothes I like and letting my hair grow?

What really matters, however, is not the way that I present myself but how others perceive me. Transition was more than a change of clothes and a lesson in make-up: those trappings were always a means to one end – being perceived to be the opposite sex. Detransition would reverse that process, and in real life, where sexed bodies matter, I have no wish to do so.

I fear a return of the mental health catastrophe that drove me to transition in the first place. So, I tread an uneasy path: I know I am not a woman, but I recognise that I need to perceive myself as a woman. And to make that work, I need others to perceive me as a woman.

At the same time, however, I certainly regret the impact on Stephanie and our children. They lost so much but gained nothing. While I never gained what I expected – womanhood – I did gain self-awareness and self-understanding. Had I not transitioned, I might still be that fearful man who had no conception of what made him tick. My energy might still be focused on keeping that beach ball below the surface – a task that would have become ever more difficult as transgender issues became so prominent. The lessons I learned maybe needed to be learned the hard way.

Perhaps one place where I can detransition is the internet? Our bodies do not need to follow us into the realms of social media, and names and avatars can be changed on a whim. There I can be she or he, and Debbie or David. But even so, why make life more difficult and store up issues when the online world crosses over into real life? Integrity matters – I am just one person and the same person in all contexts, a male transsexual.

The quasi-religious trans community from which I escaped no doubt still sees it very differently, but it's far better to be a transsexual apostate grounded in reality than a follower of their ideology, clinging desperately to that ethereal fantasy that we have a gender identity. We don't, and – what's more – it turns out we don't need one. Fulfilment is not found in identity groups, no matter how colourful the flag. It comes through self-awareness, self-understanding and self-contentment. Transition was hard work; self-discovery was harder – but infinitely more worthwhile. Why would anyone want to be defined by a transgender identity, when they could just be themselves?

EPILOGUE

ANOTHER PERSPECTIVE

by Stephanie Hayton

So where are we now? Our thirtieth wedding anniversary was in 2023: Debbie and I have known each other for most of our lives. We are friends, with a shared history and children whom we both love, but I am not romantically attracted to someone who looks like a woman. Nevertheless, we have come a long way since 2011, when Debbie first told me that the only way forward was to transition.

Initially, Debbie feared the potential devastation that transition might cause to our marriage and family. However, she joined various online trans chat groups and the messages were the same: only trans people can choose; your wife will never understand because she is 'cis'; if your wife loves you then she will affirm you. The message from the counsellor was similar: maybe Stephanie can take you shopping for female clothing? This type of 'gender affirming care' is not affirming when it imposes demands on existing relationships and people. It easily destroys the supportive networks that the trans person has with the wider world. 'Gender affirmation' draws people into a community where outsiders are the enemy: Debbie was told repeatedly that I had no say in our marriage or future.

Debbie and I talked as I tried to understand. What did she and the trans community mean by 'a woman born in a man's body'? I usually wear trousers; I am a physicist; I rarely wear make-up; but this does not make me a 'man'. Debbie could not answer. However, she repeatedly used the image of a roundabout with many exits: she thought she was still deciding which exit to choose, but it felt that she had chosen and was careering down the road at 70 mph while I struggled to catch up. Debbie could see no other way out, even if it cost us our marriage. Eventually, we agreed that Debbie would start social transitioning in December 2012. This was carefully choreographed with the children in mind: their teachers, family members and other groups were told so that they could offer support.

By April 2013, I had endured enough. It was like having two teenage girls at home: one was my fifteen-year-old daughter, but the other was aged forty-four and unmanageable. I told Debbie that our marriage could not continue because Debbie's world revolved solely around Debbie. This was the lowest point for me, but the first significant turning point back to reality for Debbie. She realised that she would lose all of us unless she started listening and allowing us to have a voice. Later, Debbie waited for my agreement before having surgery. Although I could tell that Debbie wanted to rush ahead, she was willing to wait when I said that neither I nor the children were ready.

We started to discuss other trans issues. When the government looked at the so-called 'spousal veto', Debbie initially repeated the trans-activist mantra that no cis person could stop a trans person from living as their true self. I questioned why the partner should have no say: a marriage is an agreement between two people, so why should the trans person have all the power? Surely there was a way forward which respected the rights of both in a difficult situation? Debbie started to see another perspective which recognised both parties.

Through this time, we were adjusting as a family. The children reacted differently to their dad's transition, but it was another significant milestone when each child told a friend. In the public arena, I tended to act as a single parent, attending school events and parents' evenings by myself. This way, the children did not have to answer difficult questions from classmates about their embarrassing parent! Church was different. It was a place that we continued to attend as a family. I am a lay Reader (Licensed Lay Minister) in the Church of England and juggled multiple roles. Since I was a leader, some congregation members freely shared their opinions with me. One informed me that God would not speak to me again until I was divorced. Another shared her happiness that Debbie felt able to transition. Both were equally unhelpful! Most people were confused but wanted to be kind and supportive. I was surprised how many people knew someone who knew a trans person. Even in 2012, trans people were around, fitting into society, holding down jobs, living in families, and most people accepted them.

'Fitting into society' seems to be a key principle that has been lost in the last decade of gender wars. Few people object greatly to someone who feels that they need to interact as a typical member of the opposite sex. However, I attended an LGBT event in 2012. The transwomen were easy to see because they were naturally tall and yet most still wore three-inch heels. Meanwhile, the women were smaller, and wore flat shoes. The transwomen stood out. Women know from personal experience that our naturally higher voices are less well heard and that deep voices carry better. If a transwoman's deep voice is used to dominate a conversation, particularly to speak over other women, then the transwoman is not interacting as a typical woman. Transwomen also have athletic advantages due to their male physique. If they use these benefits to win competitions against women, they are not fitting into society. People cannot expect to retain male advantage while claiming the rights of women. Yet other transwomen do not try to dominate, and do not insist on extra attention or special rights for being 'trans'. They have transitioned, sometimes many decades ago, and now have families and jobs. Their voices have been lost in recent demands that trans people should be celebrated.

Nevertheless, back in 2013, supporting the children was my priority. Although Debbie had postponed surgery, she was still on the waiting list. In November 2014, we both attended the Charing Cross Gender Clinic. The waiting room seemed full of very tall people with large hands, short skirts and anxious faces, plus Debbie and myself and two hassled receptionists. The psychiatrist was direct and fair: 'Gender surgery affects the spouses more than the children,' he said. 'Social transition affects children, but they are not interested in their parents' genitals.' Realistically, the children were adjusting to the situation. It was not easy but they loved their dad. I was the one who still juggled, adapted, managed and intervened. On one occasion, the children and I were in a local store choosing a new kitchen. The children offered their opinions on cupboards, sinks and stoves, so we sat down with a sales assistant to purchase our desired items. She was helpful and courteous. We seemed a normal family – a mother and three children choosing a new kitchen. Very stereotypical! Then Debbie joined us and handed over a credit card. There was a shift in the atmosphere. Not homophobia or transphobia; the sales assistant continued to be helpful and courteous, but we no longer fitted the stereotype. I felt like shouting, 'I am not gay!' but I could only do so by outing Debbie.

On another occasion, I was at a training course with one of Debbie's colleagues. As we finished, Debbie arrived to collect me and the colleague was surprised to see her. When Debbie pointed out that we were married, the colleague said to me, 'Oh, you look heterosexual!' Although it amused me, I wondered whether a similar comment of 'You look gay' would be seen as acceptable – or what it meant to 'look heterosexual'! Being heterosexual in a world which assumes that I am gay is a learning experience. I am learning that I can only be myself: how other people react to me often says more about them than about me. I have had to draw deeply on my faith and the sense that God had a purpose in all of this, even if I did not understand it or particularly want it.

Debbie's activism and public appearances grew. The idea of 'not outing' Debbie now seems laughable! We tried to keep her activism separate from home and family so that the children could live a relatively normal life. At one point, one son referred to himself as a 'fifteen-year-old cisgender white heterosexual male', which horrified me! At that age, they should be learning about their uniqueness, not immersed in identity language. However, as the children got older, they needed less protection. In 2018, a journalist wanted to interview Debbie for a television documentary and asked whether I could be involved. I was very reluctant: this would 'out' me as a trans spouse. Nevertheless, we spoke on the phone and she wanted the spouse's voice to be heard in the documentary. Since the spouse is often ignored, I took part. The filming took place in our dining room but, unknown to any viewers, two of our children were standing behind the cameraman, listening carefully to all that was said. The final clip was only a few minutes in an hour's programme, but this opened doors to other interviews.

By 2017, LGBT issues were a growing cause of division for the Church of England. Rather than have a small group suggest a way forward, the Church decided to facilitate a process of 'listening' to help people discuss gender, sexuality, relationships and identity. This started in 2019 under the name 'Living in Love and Faith' (LLF). The bishops were asked to recommend individuals to tell their stories and Debbie and I were interviewed, along with many others. Sixteen short 'story films' were then made and one focused on us. This was a big step for me. Suddenly, my faith, my decisions and my marriage were opened up to those who might disagree. Friends, strangers and enemies could all hear part of my journey. I felt very vulnerable, but also that, somehow, this too was part of my calling. Who I am is rooted in my experiences, choices, imperfections and faith, which tells me that God calls us to be truthful, to care, to love others as well as ourselves and to trust Him for the future. My trust was tested when there was a call to remove 'our' story film from the LLF since some trans people were upset at seeing Debbie. I was very grateful that the Church kept the film, while offering appropriate counselling to those who were upset. Removing it would have removed the voice of a trans spouse and a lay Reader.

Even now, there appear to be some strange beliefs in the trans community. In 2019, I attended a course where another attendee was a transman. After a lecture on death and dying, the transman told me that trans people did not die natural deaths because they were usually murdered. I quickly googled the statistics and pointed out that very few trans people are murdered in the UK. In fact, trans people are proportionately less likely to be murdered than women in this country. However, the transman did not believe me and repeated the assertion to the group. Everyone nodded politely, but I wondered what effect this lie was having on the mental health of individual trans people.

Living with a part-time journalist also has odd moments. On one occasion, we had to leave the house by 10.25 a.m. to catch a train. At 10.24 a.m., we were waiting in the car while Debbie finished a live interview by Zoom. With social media, responses to Debbie's views come quickly. Most reactions are positive although some are very critical, but Debbie is resilient. A few negative comments have come my way, but I ignore them where possible. We also have the occasional situation when someone will rush up and thank Debbie for her work. These can happen anywhere – on holiday, the local store, a special church service... I stand to one side and prefer to remain anonymous.

However, even now, I sometimes miss my husband. Few of us predict how our lives will go, but this is far outside any imagined prediction. By staying together, we are friends and support one another – and I have learned more than I ever expected about human sexuality and LGBT issues. In return, I have helped Debbie stay rooted in the real world rather than the mantras of the online trans community. In the real world, most people want to be kind and do not care whether someone is male or female; gay, trans or straight; old or young. Most people need to eat and sleep, and to have friends and a sense of purpose. Most people want (and many have) some self-acceptance. These are found in relationships, in communities of diverse people, and in truth.

I am grateful for those friends, teachers and relatives who have offered support over the years to us or our children by just showing acceptance. I have work that I enjoy – and my colleagues and I usually have far more pressing matters to talk about than trans issues. As our children grow into young adults, I appreciate moving into a new stage of life with Debbie where we learn to live once again as a couple without children at home. Life has been unexpected; life has its challenges; but life also offers goodness. We have come a long way... together.

ACKNOWLEDGEMENTS

I am indebted to several people without whom this book might never have seen the light of day. George Owers believed in this project from day one. As my editor, he supplied exactly the right mix of encouragement and honesty. Alex Middleton then worked wonders with the text, and his meticulous attention to detail refined and sharpened the book. I would also like to place on record my thanks to Ruth Killick, Alex Billington, and Mark Richards and the team at Forum Press.

My journey back to reality did not happen by itself. My understanding of autogynephilia and sex perception was built upon the work of others. Some are credited in the book. But I would also like to record my thanks to my friend Marcus for invaluable conversations in various pubs in several cities over the past six years. We taught each other far more than we could possibly have worked out individually.

The support of colleagues at work and in the trade union movement – too many to list here, but you know who you are – kept me going through some of the most difficult situations that I have ever faced. Friends whom I knew I could trust were like gold, and I have been blessed with so many.

Finally, I want to express my deep gratitude to my family and especially to Stephanie, my wife and best friend. Without her love and support, writing this book would have remained an impossible dream.

NOTES

2 · TRANS ORTHODOXY

1 Richard Green, 'Robert Stoller's *Sex and Gender*: 40 years on', *Archives of Sexual Behavior* 39/6 (2010), pp. 1457–65, doi: 10.1007/s10508-010-9665-5.1; Alex Byrne, 'The origin of "gender identity"', *Archives of Sexual Behavior* (2023), doi: 10.1007/s10508-023-02628-0.

2 Kelly Brewington, 'John Money, 84; doctor pioneered study of gender identity in 1950s', *Los Angeles Times* (13 July 2006), https://www.latimes.com/archives/la-xpm-2006-jul-13-me-money13-story.html.

3 'Dr Money and the boy with no penis', BBC [website] (17 September 2014), https://www.bbc.co.uk/sn/tvradio/programmes/horizon/dr_money_prog_summary.shtml.

4 Kristen Schilt, 'Harry Benjamin', *Britannica* [website], https://www.britannica.com/biography/Harry-Benjamin.

5 For the HBIGDA, see 'The Harry Benjamin International Gender Dysphoria Association (HBIGDA) Collection', Indiana University [website], https://webapp1.dlib.indiana.edu/findingaids/view?doc.view=entire_text&docId=VAC9109. For the latest iteration of the SOC, see 'Standards of care version 8', WPATH [website], https://www.wpath.org/publications/soc.

6 'Introduction to the Yogyakarta Principles', Yogyakarta Principles [website], https://yogyakartaprinciples.org/introduction/.

7 For the United Nations, see 'Human rights, sexual orientation and gender identity', RightDocs [website] (14 July 2011), https://www.right-docs.org/doc/a-hrc-res-17-19/?path=doc/a-hrc-res-17-19. For the Council of Europe, see 'Resolution 2048 (2015): discrimination against transgender people in Europe' [PDF], Parliamentary Assembly / Assemblée parlementaire [website] (2015), http://assembly.coe.int/nw/xml/xref/xref-xml2html-en.asp?fileid=21736.

8 Quoted in 'Transgender equality volume 617: debated on Thursday 1 December 2016', Parliament.uk [website] (1 December 2016), https://hansard.parliament.uk/commons/2016-12-01/debates/D4F283FB-2C02-4C8C-8C7E-BEAB889D1425/TransgenderEquality.

9 'The Harry Benjamin International Gender Dysphoria Association's standards of care for gender identity disorders, sixth version', Canadian Professional Association for Transgender Health [website] (February 2001), https://www.cpath.ca/wp-content/uploads/2009/12/WPATHsocv6.pdf.

10 Quoted in Ben Quinn, 'Petition urges Cardiff University to cancel Germaine Greer lecture', *Guardian* (23 October 2015), https://www.theguardian.com/education/2015/oct/23/petition-urges-cardiff-university-to-cancel-germain-greer-lecture.

11 Quoted ibid.

12 Julie Bindel, 'Gender benders, beware', *Guardian* (31 January 2004), https://www.theguardian.com/world/2004/jan/31/gender.weekend7.

3 · AWAKENING

1 'Westminster Social Policy Forum keynote seminar: policy priorities for transgender equality' [PDF], Westminster Forum Projects [website] (15 June 2016), https://www.westminsterforumprojects. co.uk/forums/agenda/transgender-equality-2016-agenda.pdf.

2 'House of Commons Women and Equalities Committee: transgender equality: first report of session 2015–16' [PDF], Parliament.uk [website] (8 December 2015), https://publications. parliament.uk/pa/cm201516/cmselect/cmwomeq/390/390.pdf.

3 RemakingAdam (@TransReflect), '#Transgender policy? Listen to parents #FirstDoNoHarm #silencednomore @TransMediaWatch @RichardLanderUK @DebbieHayton @mediaparents @cbbc' [Twitter post] (15 June 2016), https://twitter.com/TransReflect/ status/743037102590283776.

4 Debbie Hayton (@DebbieHayton), 'The more listening we do, the better' [Twitter post] (15 June 2016), https://twitter.com/ DebbieHayton/status/743112835698446336.

5 RemakingAdam (@TransReflect), '@DebbieHayton Yes, listen to parents inc transgendertrend.com/what-trans-act... and youthtranscriticalprofessionals.org/2016/05/30/the... Talking about #teachers' [Twitter post] (15 June 2016), https://twitter.com/ TransReflect/status/743123755837325313.

6 'What trans activism means to me as a parent', Transgender Trend [website] (14 June 2016), https://www.transgendertrend.com/what-trans-activism-means-to-me-as-a-parent/.

7 Debbie Hayton (@DebbieHayton), 'Thank you for sharing the articles. I've read them both' [Twitter post] (15 June 2016), https:// twitter.com/DebbieHayton/status/743130186154135552.

8 'Children and gender' [edition of BBC Radio 4's *Bringing Up Britain*], BBC Sounds [website] (20 July 2016), https://www.bbc.co.uk/sounds/ play/b07kq5sv. Stephanie Davies-Arai quoted at timestamp 28:38.

9 The definition is taken from Anne A. Lawrence, 'Autogynephilia: an underappreciated paraphilia', *Advances in Psychosomatic Medicine* 31 (2011), pp. 135–48, doi: 10.1159/000328921.

10 'House of Commons Women and Equalities Committee: transgender equality: first report of session 2015–16'.

11 'Resolution 2048 (2015): discrimination against transgender people in Europe' [PDF], Parliamentary Assembly / Assemblée parlementaire [website] (2015), http://assembly.coe.int/nw/xml/xref/xref-xml2html-en.asp?fileid=21736.

12 'Critically examining the doctrine of gender identity' [video of presentation by Rebecca Reilly-Cooper for Coventry Skeptics, 16 March 2016], YouTube (20 March 2016), https://www.youtube.com/watch?v=QPVNxYkawao.

13 Magdalen Berns, 'What kind of fools do Transgender UK and Stonewall take us for?' [video], YouTube (3 May 2016), https://www.youtube.com/watch?v=JkK7zisjoDk.

14 For Stonewall, see 'Our history', Stonewall [website], https://www.stonewall.org.uk/our-work/campaigns/our-history. For the Trans Advisory Group, see 'Trans Advisory Group', Stonewall [website], archived at http://web.archive.org/web/20160408152139/https://www.stonewall.org.uk/trans-advisory-group.

15 My Genderation, 'Meet Grrl Alex, the gender non conforming trans woman from Wales' [video], YouTube (16 July 2015), https://www.youtube.com/watch?v=Lj4V-Nme86U.

16 For these and all other quotations from the debate, see 'Transgender equality volume 617: debated on Thursday 1 December 2016', Parliament.uk [website] (1 December 2016), https://hansard.parliament.uk/commons/2016-12-01/debates/D4F283FB-2C02-4C8C-8C7E-BEAB889D1425/TransgenderEquality.

17 Debbie Hayton, 'Caution urged when Parliament debates changes to trans rights', Debbie Hayton [website] (29 November 2016), https://debbiehayton.com/2016/11/29/caution-urged-when-parliament-debates-changes-to-trans-rights/.

18 See karpmandramatriangle.com.

19 'Trans inmate jailed for Wakefield prison sex offences', BBC News [website] (11 October 2018), https://www.bbc.co.uk/news/uk-england-leeds-45825838.

20 Quoted in Scarlet Howes, '"I was sexually assaulted by a transgender rapist in a women's jail": female prisoner, 45, describes ordeal at the hands of sex predator, 56, who molested four inmates during three-month reign of terror', *Mail on Sunday* (15 January 2022), https://www.dailymail.co.uk/news/article-10406351/I-sexually-assaulted-transgender-rapist-womens-jail.html.

21 Miranda Yardley, 'Oppressive silence', *Morning Star* (30 June 2015), https://morningstaronline.co.uk/a-4a40-oppressive-silence-1.

22 Rebecca Reilly-Cooper, 'Redefining women: not an easy debate', *Morning Star* (15 May 2016), https://morningstaronline.co.uk/a-d93e-redefining-women-not-an-easy-debate.

23 Jennifer Duncan, 'Why I won't accept the politics of gender identity', *Morning Star* (19 May 2016), https://morningstaronline.co.uk/a-f7db-why-i-wont-accept-the-politics-of-gender-identity-1.

24 Debbie Hayton, 'How to avoid trans stereotyping?', *Morning Star* (14 April 2017), https:/morningstaronline.co.uk/a-7aa0-how-to-avoid-trans-stereotyping-1.

25 For Corbyn, see Rowena Mason, 'Let trans people self-identify their gender, Corbyn urges May', *Guardian* (19 July 2017), https://www.theguardian.com/society/2017/jul/19/let-trans-people-self-identify-gender-corbyn-urges-may.

26 Debbie Hayton, 'Self-identification & the struggle for equal rights', *Morning Star* (21 July 2017), https://www.morningstaronline.co.uk/a-cbbb-self-identification-and-the-struggle-for-equal-rights-1.

27 Lucy Bannerman, 'Transgender women criticise reform', *Times* (6 November 2017), https://www.thetimes.co.uk/article/transgender-women-criticise-reform-xtp9n6mno.

28 Debbie Hayton, 'The Gender Recognition Act needs reform but self-identification is not the answer', *Morning Star* (7 October 2017), https://morningstaronline.co.uk/article/gender-identity-debate-explored.

29 Debbie Hayton, 'We transgender women cannot self-identify our sex', *Times* (29 November 2017), https://www.thetimes.co.uk/article/we-transgender-women-cannot-self-identify-our-sex-wglh6srw3.

4 · AUTOGYNEPHILIA

1 'Transgender no longer recognised as "disorder" by WHO', BBC News [website] (29 May 2019), https://www.bbc.co.uk/news/health-48448804.

2 Ray Blanchard, 'Typology of male-to-female transsexualism', *Archives of Sexual Behavior* 14/3 (1985), pp. 247–61, doi: 10.1007/BF01542107.

3 Ray Blanchard, 'The classification and labeling of nonhomosexual gender dysphorias', *Archives of Sexual Behavior* 18/4 (1989), pp. 315–34, doi: 10.1007/BF01541951.

4 Quoted in Debbie Hayton, 'Why I became trans', UnHerd [website] (24 August 2021), https://unherd.com/2021/08/why-i-became-trans/.

5 See Steve Stewart-Williams, *The Ape that Understood the Universe: How the Mind and Culture Evolve* (Cambridge: Cambridge University Press, 2018).

6 Malte Andersson and Yoh Iwasa, 'Sexual selection', *Trends in Ecology and Evolution* 11/2 (1996), pp. 53–8, doi: 10.1016/0169-5347(96)81042-1.

7 Tim Kaiser, Marco Del Giudice and Tom Booth, 'Global sex differences in personality: replication with an open online dataset', *Journal of Personality* 88/3 (2020), pp. 415–29, doi: 10.1111/jopy.12500.

8 Nigel Barber, 'The evolutionary psychology of physical attractiveness: sexual selection and human morphology', *Ethology and Sociobiology* 16/5 (1995), pp. 395–424, doi: 10.1016/0162-3095(95)00068-2.

9 Ray Blanchard, 'Clinical observations and systematic studies of autogynephilia', *Journal of Sex and Marital Therapy* 17/4 (1991), pp. 235–51, doi: 10.1080/00926239108404348.

10 Blanchard's four strands are described in Anne A. Lawrence, 'Autogynephilia: a paraphilic model of gender identity disorder', in Jack Drescher and Ubaldo Leli (eds), *Transgender Subjectivities:*

A Clinician's Guide (New York: Haworth Medical Press, 2004), pp. 69–87, archived at https://web.archive.org/web/20150923172314/http:/www.annelawrence.com/autogynephilia,_a_paraphilic_model_of_GID.pdf.

11 Ray Blanchard, 'The concept of autogynephilia and the typology of male gender dysphoria', *Journal of Nervous and Mental Disease* 177/10 (1989), pp. 616–23, doi: 10.1097/00005053-198910000-00004.

12 For the flag, see 'Asexual Pride flag', SexualDiversity.org [website] (6 November 2022), https://www.sexualdiversity.org/edu/flags/1064.php.

13 Anne A. Lawrence, 'Becoming what we love: autogynephilic transsexualism conceptualized as an expression of romantic love', *Perspectives in Biology and Medicine* 50/4 (2007), pp. 506–20, doi: 10.1353/pbm.2007.0050.

14 J. Michael Bailey, *The Man Who Would Be Queen: The Science of Gender-Bending and Transsexualism* (Washington DC: Joseph Henry Press, 2003).

15 Alice Dreger, *Galileo's Middle Finger: Heretics, Activists, and the Search for Justice in Science* (New York: Penguin, 2015).

16 Debbie Hayton, 'I may have gender dysphoria. But I still prefer to base my life on biology, not fantasy', Quillette [website] (2 February 2020), https://quillette.com/2020/02/02/i-may-have-gender-dysphoria-but-i-still-prefer-to-base-my-life-on-biology-not-fantasy/.

5 · PERCEPTION AND REALITY

1 Matthew Moore, 'Parents condemn BBC's educational film describing 100 gender identities', *Times* (29 January 2021), https://www.thetimes.co.uk/article/parents-condemn-bbc-educational-film-describing-100-gender-identities-396092vl8.

2 'Woman billboard removed after transphobia row', BBC News [website] (26 September 2018), https://www.bbc.co.uk/news/uk-45650462.

3 'Overview: androgen insensitivity syndrome', NHS [website], https://www.nhs.uk/conditions/androgen-insensitivity-syndrome/.

4 'Corbett v Corbett (otherwise Ashley): FD 1 Feb 1970', swarb.co.uk [website], archived at https://web.archive.org/web/20130511221855/https://swarb.co.uk/corbett-v-corbett-otherwise-ashley-fd-1-feb-1970.

5 'Corbett v. Corbett (otherwise Ashley): the judgment by Justice Ormrod, February, 1970' [PDF], Press for Change [website], http://www.pfc.org.uk/caselaw/Corbett%20v%20Corbett.pdf.

6 Ibid.

7 'Change your name or personal details on your passport', Gov.uk [website], https://www.gov.uk/changing-passport-information/gender.

8 'Case of Christine Goodwin v. the United Kingdom', European Court of Human Rights [website] (11 July 2002), https://hudoc.echr.coe.int/fre#{%22itemid%22:[%22001-60596%22]}.

9 'European Convention on Human Rights' [PDF], European Court of Human Rights [website], https://www.echr.coe.int/documents/d/echr/convention_eng.

10 'Applications' [section 1 of the Gender Recognition Act 2004], Legislation.gov.uk [website], https://www.legislation.gov.uk/ukpga/2004/7/section/1.

11 'Gender reassignment' [section 7 of the Equality Act 2010], Legislation.gov.uk [website], https://www.legislation.gov.uk/ukpga/2010/15/section/7.

12 Quoted in 'Topical questions volume 721: debated on Wednesday 26 October 2022', Parliament.uk [website] (26 October 2022), https://hansard.parliament.uk/commons/2022-10-26/debates/AE123F8B-4279-4595-A046-6EB9F59E6E35/TopicalQuestions.

13 'Equality Act 2010: guidance', Gov.uk [website] (27 February 2013), https://www.gov.uk/guidance/equality-act-2010-guidance.

14 'An act relative to gender identity', 193rd General Court of the Commonwealth of Massachusetts [website] (23 November 2011), https://malegislature.gov/Laws/SessionLaws/Acts/2011/Chapter199.

15 'Trans inmate jailed for Wakefield prison sex offences', BBC News [website] (11 October 2018), https://www.bbc.co.uk/news/uk-england-leeds-45825838; 'Isla Bryson: transgender rapist jailed for eight years', BBC News [website] (28 February 2023), https://www.bbc.co.uk/news/uk-scotland-64796926.

16 See 'About us', ILGA World [website], https://ilga.org/about-us; 'Fighting for our people', Human Rights Campaign [website], https://www.hrc.org/our-work; 'About us', Stonewall [website], https://www.stonewall.org.uk/about-us.

17 For Amnesty International, see 'Gender identity for beginners: a guide to being a great trans ally', Amnesty International UK [website] (31 March 2020), https://www.amnesty.org.uk/LGBTQ-equality/gender-identity-beginners-guide-trans-allies.

18 See, for instance, Catherine Baksi, 'City law firms stick with Stonewall', *Times* (18 November 2021), https://www.thetimes.co.uk/article/city-law-firms-stick-with-stonewall-q0b3jkroc.

19 IGLYO, Thomson Reuters Foundation and Dentons, 'Only adults? Good practices in legal gender recognition for youth' [PDF], Thomson Reuters Foundation [website] (November 2019), https://www.trust.org/contentAsset/raw-data/8cf56139-c7bb-447c-babf-dd5ae56cd177/file.

20 Evelyn Richards and Rebecca Sayce, 'LGBTQ+ acronyms and terms explained – from LGBTQQIP2SAA to pansexual', *Metro* (18 November 2022), https://metro.co.uk/2022/06/07/lgbtq-terms-explained-from-gnc-and-non-binary-to-pansexual-16698689/.

21 'RUH raises Pride flag to demonstrate inclusive care for all', Royal United Hospitals Bath NHS Foundation Trust [website] (17 June 2021), https://www.ruh.nhs.uk/media/media_releases/2021_06_18_RUH_raises_Pride_flag.asp; Isabella Nikolic, 'Police paint Pride rainbows on the side of squad cars in a bid to beat online hate crimes and "give confidence to our LGBT+ community"', *Daily Mail* (22 August 2021), https://www.dailymail.co.uk/news/article-9916947/Police-paint-Pride-rainbows-squad-cars-bid-beat-online-hate-crimes.html.

22 Nikolic, 'Police paint Pride rainbows on the side of squad cars'.

23 'Artist Kev Munday adorns police car with Hampshire landmarks', BBC News [website] (7 June 2017), https://www.bbc.co.uk/news/av/uk-england-hampshire-40184610.

24 'Top 100 employers 2023', Stonewall [website], https://www.stonewall.org.uk/top-100-employers.

25 'The full list: top 100 employers 2022', Stonewall [website] (22 January 2022), archived at https://web.archive.org/web/20220223083208/https://www.stonewall.org.uk/full-list-top-100-employers-2022.

6 · GENDER IDENTITY TO GENDER APOSTASY

1 'National executive members', NASUWT [website], https://www.nasuwt.org.uk/about-us/who-s-who-at-nasuwt/national-executive-members.html.

2 'Final agenda: motions and nominations for the 150th annual Trades Union Congress 9–12 September 2018, Manchester' [PDF], TUC [website], https://www.tuc.org.uk/sites/default/files/Congress_2018_Final_Agenda.pdf.

3 'Improving the climate of debate around proposed changes to the Gender Recognition Act', *Morning Star* (4 July 2018), https://morningstaronline.co.uk/article/improving-climate-debate-around-proposed-changes-gender-recognition-act.

4 'Our history', TUC [website], https://www.tuc.org.uk/our-history.

5 'Women chainmakers', TUC [website] (10 June 2019), https://www.tuc.org.uk/news/women-chainmakers; 'How Ford's striking women drove the Equal Pay Act', TUC [website], https://www.tuc.org.uk/workplace-guidance/case-studies/how-fords-striking-women-drove-equal-pay-act.

6 Debbie Hayton, 'Self-identification will not help transgender people', *Times* (5 July 2018), https://www.thetimes.co.uk/article/self-identification-will-not-help-transgender-people-n2pm780wx;

Debbie Hayton, 'Trade unionists can help bring light and understanding to transgender debate', *Morning Star* (5 July 2018), https://morningstaronline.co.uk/article/debbie-hayton-tuc-lgbt-trans.

7 'Teaching Regulation Agency', Gov.uk [website], https://www.gov.uk/government/organisations/teaching-regulation-agency.

8 'The role of the local authority designated officer', National LADO Network [website], https://national-lado-network.co.uk/the-role-of-the-lado-local-authority-designated-officer/.

9 'Check if your dismissal is unfair', Citizens Advice [website], https://www.citizensadvice.org.uk/work/dismissal/check-your-rights-if-youre-dismissed/dismissal/check-if-your-dismissal-is-fair/.

10 'Homosexuality: the countries where it is illegal to be gay', BBC News [website] (31 March 2023), https://www.bbc.co.uk/news/world-43822234.

11 The words attributed to me here are in fact those of a blog post (now deleted) by the self-described 'transsexual male' blogger Seven Hex, which I quoted in a tweet. See Debbie Hayton (@DebbieHayton), 'By SevenHex: "Only males can be transwomen; therefore, I am male. I'm also an adult. Technically, I am a man, and no amount of hormone replacement or surgery will actually change that... this is true of all transwomen whether we like it or not."' [Twitter post] (24 January 2019), https://twitter.com/DebbieHayton/status/1088572186024165378.

12 See Debbie Hayton, 'Gender identity needs to be based on objective evidence rather than feelings', *Economist* (3 July 2018), https://www.economist.com/open-future/2018/07/03/gender-identity-needs-to-be-based-on-objective-evidence-rather-than-feelings.

13 Debbie Hayton, 'Aggressive protests like that in Brighton mean the real causes of transphobia go unaddressed', *Morning Star* (5 October 2019), https://morningstaronline.co.uk/article/f/making-sense-trans-rights.

14 Debbie Hayton (@DebbieHayton), 'My latest for @M_Star_ Online: 'Trans women are biologically male – in fact being male is the sole qualifying criteria to be a trans woman – and women are biologically female. Male people are not female people and therefore trans women are not women. Those are the facts' [Twitter post] (5 October 2019), https://twitter.com/DebbieHayton/status/1180434241777258501?s=17.

7 · APOSTASY AND EXCLUSION

1 Andrew Pakes (@andrewpakes), 'This is a great picture. @The_TUC @TUCEquality #LGBT committee resolute in its support for #trans rights. Rights are always claimed, not given. We are always better together @stonewalluk' [Twitter post] (17 October 2019), archived at https://archive.ph/3r3jL.
2 Met Contact Centre (@MetCC), 'Hi, was this reported at the time? If not it can be reported here...' [Twitter post] (6 December 2019), https://twitter.com/MetCC/status/1202854437741563904.
3 'Trans rights position statement', NASUWT [website] (4 April 2022), https://www.nasuwt.org.uk/advice/equalities/under-represented-groups/lgbti-teachers/trans-rights-position-statement.html.
4 Debbie Hayton, 'Caution urged when Parliament debates changes to trans rights', Debbie Hayton [website] (29 November 2016), https://debbiehayton.com/2016/11/29/caution-urged-when-parliament-debates-changes-to-trans-rights/.

8 · TERF ISLAND: BRITAIN AGAINST THE WORLD

1 IGLYO, Thomson Reuters Foundation and Dentons, 'Only adults? Good practices in legal gender recognition for youth' [PDF], Thomson Reuters Foundation [website] (November 2019), https://www.trust.org/contentAsset/raw-data/8cf56139-c7bb-447c-babf-dd5ae56cd177/file.

2 For the report, see 'House of Commons Women and Equalities Committee: transgender equality: first report of session 2015–16'[PDF], Parliament.uk [website] (8 December 2015), https://publications. parliament.uk/pa/cm201516/cmselect/cmwomeq/390/390.pdf.

3 Quoted in Lucy Fisher, 'Switching gender to be made easier', *Times* (24 July 2017), https://www.thetimes.co.uk/article/switching-gender-to-be-made-easier-j97h2tfgg.

4 'About', Woman's Place UK [website], https://womansplaceuk. org/about/; 'We are Woman's Place UK', Woman's Place UK [website], https://womansplaceuk.org/2020/02/11/we-are-womans-place-uk/.

5 Jen Izakson, 'Misogynist violence at Speakers' Corner', *Morning Star* (19 September 2017), https://morningstaronline.co.uk/article/misogynist-violence-speakers%E2%80%99-corner.

6 'Transgender activist Tara Wolf fined £150 for assaulting "exclusionary" radical feminist in Hyde Park', *Standard* (13 April 2018), https://www.standard.co.uk/news/crime/transgender-activist-tara-wolf-fined-ps150-for-assaulting-exclusionary-radical-feminist-in-hyde-park-a3813856.html. For the video evidence, see Miranda Yardley, 'Clear footage of the assault on a woman by transgender activists at Speakers' Corner' [video], YouTube (15 September 2017), https://www.youtube.com/watch?v=9_d3ozhSE-U.

7 Kevin Courtney (@cyclingkev), 'I decided to come and see what the @Womens_Place_UK meeting was all about tonight. The protestors outside are banging on the windows so loud that you can't hear yourself think inside. That can't be the right way to deal with the issue #WPUKLab19' [Twitter post] (23 September 2019), https://twitter.com/cyclingkev/status/1176197248667082752.

8 Kevin Courtney (@cyclingkev), 'The @women's_place_uk meeting is coming to an end. I'm very pleased to have come. I've heard opinions that the protestors wouldn't agree with. I haven't heard any hate speech. When the speeches are put online in time I will share links so you can judge for yourself #WPUKLab19'

[Twitter post] (23 September 2019), https://twitter.com/cyclingkev/status/1176221606852648962.

9 'Women's meeting besieged by raging crowd', *Morning Star* (24 September 2019), https://morningstaronline.co.uk/article/f/wpuk-fringe-report.

10 Fair Play for Women [website], https://fairplayforwomen.com.

11 Transgender Trend [website], https://www.transgendertrend.com.

12 Sex Matters [website], https://sex-matters.org.

13 Quoted in 'Maya Forstater: woman loses tribunal over transgender tweets', BBC News [website] (19 December 2019), https://www.bbc.co.uk/news/uk-50858919.

14 Helen Joyce, *Trans: When Ideology Meets Reality* (London: Oneworld, 2021); 'Helen Joyce joins Sex Matters as director of advocacy', Sex Matters [website] (1 April 2022), https://sex-matters.org/posts/updates/helen-joyce-joins/.

15 For Women Scotland [website], https://forwomen.scot; Murray Blackburn Mackenzie [website], https://murrayblackburnmackenzie.org.

16 'Sex' [section 11 of the Equality Act 2010], Legislation.gov.uk [website], https://www.legislation.gov.uk/ukpga/2010/15/section/11.

17 Quoted in 'Nicola Sturgeon's gender conundrum: is Isla Bryson a man or a woman?', BBC News [website] (10 February 2023), https://www.bbc.co.uk/news/uk-scotland-64590421.

18 'General' [section 9 of the Gender Recognition Act 2004], Legislation.gov.uk [website], https://www.legislation.gov.uk/ukpga/2004/7/section/9.

19 'Peerages etc.' [section 16 of the Gender Recognition Act 2004], Legislation.gov.uk [website], https://www.legislation.gov.uk/ukpga/2004/7/section/16.

20 'Schedule 4: effect on marriage' [part of the Gender Recognition Act 2004], Legislation.gov.uk [website], https://www.legislation.gov.uk/ukpga/2004/7/schedule/4.

21 'Part 7: separate and single services. Separate services for the sexes' [part of the Equality Act 2010], Legislation.gov.uk [website], https://www.legislation.gov.uk/ukpga/2010/15/notes/division/3/16/20/7.

22 'Gender Recognition Reform (Scotland) Bill: cabinet secretary's statement', Scottish Government [website] (3 March 2022), https://www.gov.scot/publications/gender-recognition-reform-scotland-bill-cabinet-secretarys-statement/.

23 'Opinion of Lady Haldane in petition of For Women Scotland Limited' [PDF], Scottish Courts and Tribunals [website] (13 December 2022), https://www.scotcourts.gov.uk/docs/default-source/cos-general-docs/pdf-docs-for-opinions/2022csoh90.pdf?sfvrsn=8eee302c_1.

24 'Gender representation objective' [section 1 of the Gender Representation on Public Boards (Scotland) Act 2018], Legislation.gov.uk [website], https://www.legislation.gov.uk/asp/2018/4/section/1/enacted.

25 'Key definitions' [section 2 of the Gender Representation on Public Boards (Scotland) Act 2018], Legislation.gov.uk [website], https://www.legislation.gov.uk/asp/2018/4/section/2/enacted.

26 'Opinion of Lady Haldane in petition of For Women Scotland Limited'.

27 On the 'family-friendly' Scottish parliament, see Jenni Davidson, 'The mother of all parliaments: how family friendly is Holyrood really?', *Holyrood* (13 May 2021), https://www.holyrood.com/inside-politics/view,the-mother-of-all-parliaments-how-family-friendly-is-holyrood.

28 IGLYO, Thomson Reuters Foundation and Dentons, 'Only adults? Good practices in legal gender recognition for youth'.

29 'Male-bodied transgender inmate housed with women', *Law Society of Ireland Gazette* (18 October 2019), https://www.lawsociety.ie/gazette/top-stories/2019/10-october/male-bodied-transgender-inmate-housed-with-women-prisoners.

30 'Prison Service Dáil Éireann debate, Tuesday – 25 April 2023', Tithe an Oireachtas / House of the Oireachtas [website] (25 April 2023), https://www.oireachtas.ie/en/debates/question/2023-04-25/419/.

31 Quoted in 'Male-bodied transgender inmate housed with women'.

32 'Tiffany Scott: call to block trans prisoner's move to women's jail', BBC News [website] (28 January 2023), https://www.bbc.co.uk/news/uk-scotland-64438457.

33 Quoted in an attachment to MurrayBlackburnMackenzie (@mbmpolicy), 'Hello, the extract from our paper, and the full reference is here: Morton, J. (2018). 'A Scottish History of Trans Equality Activism' in (ed.) Burns, C. 'Trans Britain. Our Journey from the Shadows.' Unbound: London' [Twitter post] (10 January 2022), https://twitter.com/mbmpolicy/status/1480626758353399814.

34 For Speak Up for Women, see Speak Up for Women [website], https://www.speakupforwomen.nz. For the New Zealand bill, see 'Births, Deaths, Marriages, and Relationships Registration Bill', New Zealand Parliament [website] (9 March 2023), https://bills.parliament.nz/v/6/6e9cd69c-7b09-41b4-b5f9-98d2f73fbb64?Tab=history, and specifically '22A Eligibility to apply for registration of nominated sex' [part of Births, Deaths, Marriages, and Relationships Registration Bill], New Zealand Legislation [website], https://www.legislation.govt.nz/bill/government/2017/0296/latest/LMS518655.html. See also Debbie Hayton, 'New Zealand's worrying battle over transgender rights', *Spectator* (3 July 2021), https://www.spectator.co.uk/article/new-zealand-s-worrying-battle-over-transgender-rights/.

35 My translation. See '¿Por qué surge esta alianza?', Contra el Borrado de las Mujeres [website], https://contraelborradodelasmujeres.org.

36 LBC (@LBC), '"Outside of the UK, we are known as the transphobia capital of the world. We're often referred to as TERF island." Natasha Devon's passionate reaction as the Council of Europe condemns the UK's "virulent attacks" on LGBTI rights' [Twitter post] (6 February 2022), https://twitter.com/LBC/status/1490424440454369281?lang=en.

37 Quotations taken from Ben Hunte, 'Trans people say they're leaving England because of non-stop transphobia', Vice [website] (18 January 2023), https://www.vice.com/en/article/qjkqn7/trans-people-leaving-england.

38 For the expulsion of the Russian Federation, see 'The Russian Federation is excluded from the Council of Europe', Council of Europe [website] (16 March 2022), https://www.coe.int/en/web/portal/-/the-russian-federation-is-excluded-from-the-council-of-europe.

39 'A convention to protect your rights and liberties', Council of Europe [website] (16 March 2022) https://www.coe.int/en/web/human-rights-convention.

40 'Resolution 2048 (2015): discrimination against transgender people in Europe' [PDF], Parliamentary Assembly / Assemblée parlementaire [website] (2015), http://assembly.coe.int/nw/xml/xref/xref-xml2html-en.asp?fileid=21736.

41 Fourat Ben Chikha, 'Combating rising hate against LGBTI people in Europe' [PDF], Parliamentary Assembly / Assemblée parlementaire [website] (27 September 2021), https://assembly.coe.int/LifeRay/EGA/Pdf/TextesProvisoires/2021/20210921-RisingHateLGBTI-EN.pdf. For Fourat Ben Chikha, see 'Mr Fourat Ben Chikha (Belgium, SOC)', Parliamentary Assembly / Assemblée parlementaire [website], https://pace.coe.int/en/members/8133/ben-chikha.

42 'Sénateurs actuels (alphabétique)', Sénat de Belgique [website], https://www.senate.be/www/?MIval=/index_senate&MENUID=11200&LANG=fr.

43 'Combating rising hate against LGBTI people in Europe: doc. 15425: compendium of written amendments', Parliamentary

Assembly / Assemblée parlementaire [website] (24 September 2021), https://pace.coe.int/en/files/29418/compendium.

44 For Antoniazzi's speech, see PACE, '25 Jan 2022 – a.m. – 3rd sitting – PACE "hybrid" winter plenary session' [video], YouTube (25 January 2022), https://www.youtube.com/watch?v=gNqZHreBP7Y&t=5818s.

45 'What is ILGA-Europe', ILGA-Europe [website], archived at http://web.archive.org/web/20220218080059/https://www.ilga-europe.org/who-we-are/what-ilga-europe.

46 For Lord Foulkes's intervention, see PACE, '25 Jan 2022 – a.m. – 3rd sitting – PACE "hybrid" winter plenary session' [video], YouTube (25 January 2022), https://www.youtube.com/watch?v=gNqZHreBP7Y&t=8100s.

47 For Corbyn, see PACE, '25 Jan 2022 – a.m. – 3rd sitting – PACE "hybrid" winter plenary session' [video], YouTube (25 January 2022), https://www.youtube.com/watch?v=gNqZHreBP7Y&t=8425s. For Lord Howell, see PACE, '25 Jan 2022 – a.m. – 3rd sitting – PACE "hybrid" winter plenary session' [video], YouTube (25 January 2022), https://www.youtube.com/watch?v=gNqZHreBP7Y&t=8471s.

48 For Lord Blencathra, see '25 Jan 2022 – a.m. – 3rd sitting – PACE "hybrid" winter plenary session' [video], YouTube (25 January 2022), https://www.youtube.com/watch?v=gNqZHreBP7Y&t=6020s. See also Debbie Hayton, 'Stop saying the UK is transphobic', UnHerd [website] (27 January 2022), https://unherd.com/2022/01/stop-pretending-the-uk-is-transphobic/.

9 · CHILDREN AND TECHNOLOGY

1 'Ignatius of Antioch: power and freedom in the early Church', Christian History for Everyman [website], https://www.christian-history.org/ignatius.html.

2 'Myers–Briggs type indicator (MBTI)', Myers–Briggs Company [website], https://www.themyersbriggs.com/en-US/Products-and-Services/Myers-Briggs.

3 'Gender distributions on MBTI domains' [table], https://www.researchgate.net/figure/Gender-Distributions-on-MBTI-Domains_tbl1_249827418. Taken from Tracy Cross, Kristie Neumeister and Jerrell Cassady, 'Psychological types of academically gifted adolescents', *Gifted Child Quarterly* 51/3 (2007), doi: 10.1177/0016986207302723.

4 Adrian Furnham and Luke Treglown, 'Sex differences in personality scores on six scales: many significant, but mostly small, differences', *Current Psychology* 42/9 (2023), pp. 3449–59, doi: 10.1007/s12144-021-01675-x.

5 Charles Arthur, 'Half of UK population owns a smartphone', *Guardian* (31 October 2011), https://www.theguardian.com/technology/2011/oct/31/half-uk-population-owns-smartphone.

6 'The communications market 2016: 5 – internet and online content' [PDF], Ofcom [website], https://www.ofcom.org.uk/__data/assets/pdf_file/0023/26393/uk_internet.pdf.

7 'Coronavirus: UK schools, colleges and nurseries to close from Friday', BBC News [website] (18 March 2020), https://www.bbc.co.uk/news/uk-51952314.

8 'WHO director-general's opening remarks at the media briefing on COVID-19 – 11 March 2020', World Health Organization [website] (11 March 2020), https://www.who.int/director-general/speeches/detail/who-director-general-s-opening-remarks-at-the-media-briefing-on-covid-19---11-march-2020.

9 Rowan Williams et al., 'On the ban on conversion therapy excluding trans people' [PDF] (4 April 2022), https://static1.squarespace.com/static/5788afd615d5db91c69f8879/t/624b0656db1aa213c819e82f/1649083990974/Letter+to+the+Prime+Minister+4.4.22.pdf. See also Gabriella Swerling, 'Becoming transgender a sacred journey of becoming whole, says ex-Archbishop of Canterbury', *Telegraph* (4 April 2022), https://www.telegraph.co.uk/news/2022/04/04/becoming-transgender-sacred-journey-becoming-whole-says-ex-archbishop/.

10 Matthew Roberts, 'The religion of self-worship', The Critic [website] (7 April 2022), https://thecritic.co.uk/the-religion-of-self-worship/.

11 Polly Carmichael, Gary Butler, Una Masic, Tim J. Cole, Bianca L. De Stavola, Sarah Davidson, Elin M. Skageberg, Sophie Khadr and Russell M. Viner, 'Short-term outcomes of pubertal suppression in a selected cohort of 12 to 15 year old young people with persistent gender dysphoria in the UK', *PLoS ONE* 16/2 (2021), e0243894, doi: 10.1371/journal.pone.0243894.

12 James Reinl, 'Exclusive: Miami sex-change surgeon who dubs herself "Dr Teetus Deletus" is reported to consumer watchdog for "deceptively" luring "vulnerable" teens into transgender operations with gimmicky TikTok video blitz', *Daily Mail* (13 October 2022), https://www.dailymail.co.uk/news/article-11303919/Florida-sex-change-surgeon-dubs-Dr-Teetus-Deletus-REPORTED-consumer-watchdog.html.

13 'Sexual and reproductive health terms understanding sex, gender, orientation and expression: the genderbread person' [PDF], University of Washington [website], https://depts.washington.edu/edgh/zw/hit/web/project-resources/SRH_terms.pdf; 'Gender unicorn', Trans Student Educational Resources [website], https://transstudent.org/gender/.

14 Ibid.

15 'Best practice, toolkits and resources', Stonewall [website], https://www.stonewall.org.uk/best-practice-toolkits-and-resources-0.

16 See https://karpmandramatriangle.com.

10 · THE TRANSSEXUAL FUTURE

1 'List of LGBTQ+ terms', Stonewall [website], https://www.stonewall.org.uk/list-lgbtq-terms.

2 'LGBTQ+ glossary', PFLAG [website], https://pflag.org/glossary/.

3 See 'Determination of applications' [section 2 of the Gender Recognition Act 2004], Legislation.gov.uk [website], https://www.legislation.gov.uk/ukpga/2004/7/section/2.

4 Debbie Hayton, 'Caution urged when Parliament debates changes to trans rights', Debbie Hayton [website] (29 November 2016), https://debbiehayton.com/2016/11/29/caution-urged-when-parliament-debates-changes-to-trans-rights/.

5 'Equality Act 2010', Legislation.gov.uk [website], https://www.legislation.gov.uk/ukpga/2010/15/contents.

6 'Campaign update: make the Equality Act clear', Sex Matters [website] (1 June 2023), https://sex-matters.org/posts/updates/campaign-update-make-the-equality-act-clear/.

7 'Why we don't want "biological" added before "sex" in the law', Sex Matters [website] (30 May 2023), https://sex-matters.org/posts/single-sex-services/why-we-dont-want-biological-added-before-sex-in-the-law/.

8 Kemi Badenoch's words are quoted in 'Topical questions volume 721: debated on Wednesday 26 October 2022', Parliament.uk [website] (26 October 2022), https://hansard.parliament.uk/commons/2022-10-26/debates/AE123F8B-4279-4595-A046-6EB9F59E6E35/TopicalQuestions.

9 For the Act, see 'Gender Recognition Act 2004', Legislation.gov.uk [website], https://www.legislation.gov.uk/ukpga/2004/7/contents.

10 'European Convention on Human Rights' [PDF], European Court of Human Rights [website], https://www.echr.coe.int/documents/d/echr/convention_eng.

11 'Marriage (Same Sex Couples) Act 2013', Legislation.gov.uk [website], https://www.legislation.gov.uk/ukpga/2013/30/contents/enacted/data.htm.